D1557622

The Good News of Revelation

The Good News
of Revelation

By LARRY HELYER
and ED CYZEWSKI

CASCADE *Books* · Eugene, Oregon

THE GOOD NEWS OF REVELATION

Cascade Books
An Imprint of Wipf and Stock Publishers
199 W. 8th Ave., Suite 3
Eugene, OR 97401

www.wipfandstock.com

ISBN 13: 978-1-62032-629-9

Cataloguing-in-Publication Data

Helyer, Larry

The good news of Revelation / Larry Helyer and Ed Cyzewski

xvi + 102 p. ; 23 cm. Includes bibliographical references.

ISBN 13: 978-1-62032-629-9

1. Bible. Revelation—Criticism, interpretation, etc. 2. Bible. Revelation—Hermeneutics. I. Cyzewski, Ed. II. Title.

BS2825.5 G75 2014

Manufactured in the U.S.A.

Larry's Dedication

This book is dedicated to my daughter Alicia and my son Nate. May they continue "to follow the Lamb wherever he goes" (Rev 14:4).

Ed's Dedication

For my professors who taught me that scripture is to be revered, not feared—even the book of Revelation.

Contents

Preface

WRITING ANYTHING DEFINITIVE ABOUT a perplexing book like Revelation is no small task. However, harmonizing the views of two writers about this book of the Bible is particularly daunting. As Larry and I have worked on this project together, our mutual goal all along has been presenting a clear picture of the good news of Christ in the book of Revelation and offering alternatives to some of the more popular interpretations of Revelation. We each approach Revelation with slightly different views about some of the details, but we are in agreement that it offers us a hopeful message about the sufficiency of the cross and resurrection to defeat evil, as well as presenting the future hope of the church when Christ returns.

Any ambiguity over difficult theological issues in Revelation should be chalked up to the challenge of merging our two perspectives into a single book. Larry has written about the book of Revelation at length in his book *Revelation for Dummies* that provides a reliable introduction to his own views and a far more complete overview than this brief study. I highly recommend it to all who wish to study Revelation further.

We hope that this book will open the eyes of our readers to the hope and encouragement in a book of the Bible that has historically stirred up anxiety. May the comfort from the risen Christ, our loving Father, and the indwelling Spirit rest upon you as you read about the good news of Revelation.

—Ed Cyzewski

Acknowledgments

This project would have never come together without the insight, experience, and hard work of Larry Helyer. Each chapter is deeper and more instructive because of his rigorous research and practical insights. He also nurtured my interest in Jewish apocalyptic literature in my undergraduate days at Taylor University and graciously allowed me to research and edit with him on his intertestamental literature book. I number him among the most influential people who have shaped the course of my life.

I'm grateful for the work of the team at Cascade: Rodney, Diane, Chris, Justin, and Laura, to name those I've worked with directly. Karen Neumair faithfully worked to make this project the best it could be and has been a staunch advocate for it, going above and beyond the call of duty time and time again.

My friends, blog readers, and newsletter subscribers have been a tremendous encouragement as they read early drafts and offered their feedback. Though I've surely forgotten some of you, I'd like to thank Kurt Willems, Tanya Marlow, Mike Morrell, Emily Miller, Laurie McClary, Preston Yancey, Derek Cooper, Zack Hunt, and Kelly J. Youngblood.

My long-suffering wife Julie has endured many long conversations about what I hoped this book would be, and she always asked the perfect question or gave the feedback I needed. Julie, I'm grateful that you support me in every way possible as a writer and that so much of what's good about this book reflects our interactions and your support.

—Ed Cyzewski

This book originated in Ed Cyzewski's vision and initiative. What a pleasure to work with a gifted, former student on such a project! I feel like I'm just hanging on to the coat tails of Ed's expertise and savvy in the new age of blogging, Facebook, Twitter, and the like. Thanks too, Ed, for judiciously updating some of my generational prose.

Like Ed, I acknowledge with gratitude the work of the editorial team at Cascade and our literary agent, Karen Neumair. Books have always been communal undertakings!

There have been many shaping influences in my scholarly development. I wish to single out one person in particular who left an important imprint. Dr. Ralph P. Martin, former Professor of New Testament at Fuller Theological Seminary, was not only a mentor but a friend. He went to be with the Lord February 25, 2013. May his memory be blessed!

My wife, Joyce, has graciously allowed me to spend uninterrupted hours in front of my computer. She is a precious gift from the Lord and I don't tell her that often enough (Prov 19:14).

 —Larry Helyer

Introduction:
A Story Misunderstood

THE BOOK OF REVELATION has been terrifying and tantalizing readers for years with its accounts of water turning to blood, evil beasts rising from the sea, and plagues wiping out most of humanity. How in the world could anyone call it good news? The very thought of describing such an odd book as "good" strikes the casual reader today as impossible. If Revelation is predicting the future, as it seems to be doing, then we're all in for it one day.

However, there is substantial evidence suggesting that if you read Revelation as a calendar of events precisely predicting the end of the world, you've probably misunderstood what it's all about. The images, themes, and stories used in Revelation are common to the Bible, especially portions of the Old Testament prophetic books, and to Jewish literature written around the same time as the book of Revelation. All of these clues suggest a very different way of reading this challenging book.

The lessons that we draw from these comparisons help us arrive at a fresh understanding of Revelation. Above all, you'll arrive at a rather startling discovery: Revelation is an encouraging book with good news, especially for people who are suffering.

That may be hard to imagine, and therefore, we'll lead off each section with a chapter that offers a fictional short story that will portray how the author and original audience of Revelation may have viewed this unusual book. These fictional characters and scenes will help you grasp how Revelation could have taken shape in its original setting as a message of hope. In addition, after each fictional chapter, we'll follow it with a chapter that provides a more focused study of what Revelation has to say about that section's particular theme.

We'll be the first to admit that our chapters that reimagine the original setting of Revelation aren't quite as exciting as some more recent works that describe Revelation being fulfilled in the present or near future. It's tough to compete with attack helicopters and car chases. What we lack in drama, we hope to compensate with comfort and insight to people who are in need of good news.

Revelation is often interpreted as an end-times blood bath in which an angry God comes to destroy the world. Does this really capture the message of a book written to people who were suffering severe persecution? The book of Revelation itself indicates that God's ultimate purpose is to make "all things new" (Rev 21:5). The Jesus some imagine in Revelation misses some of the key qualities we find in the Jesus of the Gospels who weeps over Jerusalem or the God who declared that his creation was good. Doesn't it make sense to seek a way of connecting Revelation with the rest of the Bible and with its original context? Can Revelation help us understand God's mercy and justice, God's patience and power?

Thankfully, there is a way to make sense of Revelation so that it fits the story of the Bible and makes perfect sense for its original audience. In short, that's what this book is all about. We think you'll be greatly encouraged by what you read.

We have divided this book into five sections. The first section will give you an overview of Revelation, including an explanation of how Revelation fits into the literature of its day. Each of the following sections will then address a major theme in Revelation: perseverance, justice, the battle between good and evil, and hope for the future.

We begin our journey into the book of Revelation in a dark cave on an island just off the coast of Turkey.

SECTION 1

How to Start an Apocalypse

Chapter 1

An Exile to the Rescue

Was it real or just a vision? Whichever it was, it left John exhausted and troubled.

Speaking of visions, John never would have foreseen he'd tire of eating fish, but then again the monotony of overcooked fish in prison could try the tastes of any old man. He often reminded himself that he was in exile, not prison. Somehow spending his days in a cave on a desolate island should have consoled him. So many had been locked behind bars and beaten, while others had been thrown to the wild beasts in other parts of the empire. He was lucky, wasn't he?

Picking at his charred chunk of fish, he mulled over the vision he'd just had with beasts, bowls, angels, and a bejeweled city falling from the sky—or did he actually see it all? As a follower of Jesus, he thought he could handle the strange and unusual. He'd grown used to seeing the sick healed, the dead raised, and the demons cast out. Why should these visions disturb him so?

He tried to push it out of his mind while he ate. He was thankful for his food. Knots in his stomach made it hard for him to swallow. He coughed. No, he wouldn't be able to eat much of anything until he figured out what to do with this vision—or experience. Exasperated, he sighed and pushed his fish away.

Did the risen Christ really speak to him?

It had to be true. He was sure at the time that he was standing next to an angel. He was sure he had heard the thunderous voice of the risen and exalted Jesus. It had been just like the time he'd stood on the mountain with

Jesus as a young man. Moses and Elijah had overwhelmed him with their shining splendor, driving home his unworthiness to stand before the messengers of a holy God. The angels by the empty tomb of Jesus had appeared as young men, powerful and beautiful, but very ordinary. But this vision had been so very different from all of the others. The angelic guide spoke in riddles, took him on a journey through heaven, revealed spiritual battles, and showed him the heavenly city of Jerusalem descending to earth. It all began to make sense—the vision was telling him about the ultimate victory of God's people over the forces of darkness.

Tears welled up in John's eyes. Could the people of Jesus in the seven churches possibly survive such a devastating onslaught by Satan and his army? And yet, in his visions, a great multitude stood before the throne of God and the Lamb, lifting their praise and thanksgiving. God is faithful! They were not abandoned, even as the bruises and scars on Jesus' body spoke of the suffering many continued to endure.

As he recalled the vision of the New Jerusalem descending to earth, his body warmed with the presence of God. The ancient people of Israel lived on in the people of Jesus, and soon God would restore his people. Though Rome might take everything the Jesus followers could claim on this earth— even their lives—God wasn't finished yet; he would never abandon or forsake his people. The dark, damp cave that acted as his prison was not his last stop as a follower of Jesus.

Yes, though Rome has the upper hand now, God has the last word. The New Jerusalem will come to earth, the dead will be raised, and the followers of Jesus will rule over the world. As he dried his tears, John laughed at the seeming foolishness of it all. How many would think he was a delirious old man for thinking such things? Everywhere he looked, God seemed to be losing. The persecutions were terrible and many apostles had been martyred

And yet hope continued to burn within his chest. Leaning forward to pray with his lips pressed to the cool rock of his cave, John whispered, "Speak Lord, your servant is listening."

The idea hit him like a bolt of lightning. He rose to his feet with unknown strength. He settled at his small table by the entrance to the cave. A ship coasted into the harbor down below. It was a clear day with blue skies, and the sun baked the workers in the fields and rock quarry. Though it was a perfect day, he would stay inside.

He had to write a message of encouragement to the brothers and sisters in the house churches of Asia, telling them to hold on. Though Greek wasn't his mother tongue, over the years he had acquired a basic fluency and had already, with the help of the Holy Spirit, been able to compose a gospel and three letters in the Greek language. This prophecy, however, was something quite different. He needed to convey the content of his visions in a way that would both make sense to his readers and escape the attention of the Roman officials on the mainland. A prophetic letter would soon be confiscated and destroyed if it predicted the fall of Rome.

He remembered the books he'd read years ago where great spiritual leaders such as Moses and Enoch took heavenly journeys and witnessed symbolic events that explained the workings of God in the present. This could work. He would adopt many of the conventions of Jewish apocalyptic writings that used coded symbols and images. The believers would be able to read through the thinly veiled codes encouraging them to hold on and persevere in the midst of their sufferings.

He would write his apocalypse, a revelation, in a way that "insiders" would get the message. The good news would be trumpeted to the faithful: God wins in the end, and he will raise his people to new life! No earthly or spiritual power could stop God's plan from unfolding. John just hoped he could keep it short.

Chapter 2

Getting Our Bearings

IN THIS CHAPTER

- Revelation as three types of literature.
- The historical setting of Revelation.
- An outline of Revelation.

THE BOOK OF REVELATION unloads overwhelming and bewildering images on readers: candlesticks, seals, trumpets, bowls, beasts, angels, and other creatures that defy explanation. Trying to make sense of this book presents major challenges. What in the world is going on here? Like putting the pieces of a puzzle together, we need to pause a moment to look at the entire picture. What are we looking at? What exactly was John trying to give us?

SEEING THE PARTS OF THE WHOLE

We suggest that the book can be broken down into four major sections that start with an opening and wrap up with a conclusion as illustrated in the following outline.

1:1–8	Opening
1:9–20	Inaugural Vision
2–3	Letters to the Seven Churches

GETTING A FEEL FOR THE KIND OF BOOK WE'RE READING

A very important question must now be considered: What kind of writing is this? The answer is not a straightforward choice. In fact, Revelation is unique in the New Testament in that it demonstrates the characteristics of *three different kinds of writing.*

Epistle

Revelation clearly possesses some attributes normally associated with a letter. For example, the first chapter (vv. 3–9) displays the typical features of a first century AD letter opening:

1. Name of the author (John)

2. Recipients (the seven churches of the province of Asia)

3. Greetings (verses 4c–5a)

4. Doxology (verses 5b–6)

Furthermore, in chapters 2 through 3, John sends seven short letters or messages to seven churches in the Roman province of Asia. Finally, the book concludes with a benediction, so typical of Paul's letters ("The grace of the Lord Jesus be with God's people. Amen.").

> It's important to remember that in the first century AD, books were in scroll format. That is, they were sheets of papyrus (an ancient version of paper) or animal skins on which writing was inscribed with ink and which had to be unrolled in order to read and rolled back up again when finished. A scroll had a practical length limit since a very long scroll would be too cumbersome to handle. The longest scroll in the famous library at Qumran, the scroll of Isaiah, is about 24 feet long when fully stretched out. The book of Revelation would only have been about six feet long.

Prophecy

On the other hand, it's obvious that most of this book has a quite different feel to it than a letter. In fact, the author John actually calls the scroll a "prophecy" (1:3; 22:7, 10, 18–19).

When John calls his scroll a prophecy, he is using a form of writing well known in the Old Testament. *Prophecy is preaching about essential truths aimed at the conscience of the reader or listener.* In the Old Testament, prophecy typically addressed the basics of living as God's people: worshipping God alone and leaving behind idols.

> Most people in the first century lacked the necessary skills to read. Consequently, early Christian letters were read aloud at the meetings of the believers. This is clearly the case with the Apostle Paul's letters to various Christian congregations (1 Thessalonians 5:27; Colossians 4:16). A special blessing is promised both for the person who reads aloud the book of Revelation to the assembled believers and the listeners who put in practice what is written (Revelation 1:3).

To be sure, prophecy did occasionally refer to what the Lord determined to do in the future. Sometimes, predictive prophecy was given in order to confirm the word of the Lord spoken through the prophet. We can summarize this by saying that, for the most part, prophecy was inspired speech that appealed to the listeners to repent and to put their complete trust in the Lord. This inspired preaching sometimes revealed God's future plans, whether in the near or distant future. The Old Testament prophetic books, especially Isaiah, Jeremiah, Ezekiel, Daniel, Joel, and Zechariah are the single most important models for what John writes in the book of Revelation. In fact, we will repeatedly refer to passages from these Old Testament prophets as we work our way through this book. However, calling Revelation a prophetic book does not always mean it's giving us a blueprint of the future.

Apocalyptic

There is, however, one more type of writing that clearly leaves a discernible mark on the book of Revelation. For some four hundred years, in Jewish and Christian circles, a form of writing called "apocalyptic" flourished. *Apocalyptic derives from the word apocalypse, meaning an unveiling or revelation.* An apocalypse typically displays the following characteristics:

1. Reveals both end-time events (especially the final triumph of good over evil) and spiritual realities in the present not accessible to the physical senses.

2. Communicates by means of a wide range of assorted figures, symbols, and images through visionary experiences.

3. Explains the meaning of visions and symbols by means of an angelic informant.

4. Maintains a clear separation between good and evil and urges the reader/listener to choose which side he or she is on.

5. Assumes those in the know can decode the message.

6. Leaves outsiders clueless as to what is going on and what is going to happen.

7. Insists the end times are about to happen.

John adopts these features of apocalyptic literature in order to urge his Christian audience in the seven Asian churches to be faithful in the face of persecution and suffering and to trust unreservedly in the God who ultimately delivers us from all evil (Matt 6:13).

In short, the book of Revelation is a unique form of writing, incorporating three distinct formats, focusing on a unique person, the Lord Jesus Christ, and ending in a unique plan for the entire universe. Coming as it does at the conclusion of the Bible, this book brings together the leading themes of Scripture in a most fitting finale.

OPENING (REVELATION 1:1–8)

Beginnings are always important, especially in a book like this. The first eight verses announce the primary theme of the book, which is easily spotted in v. 7: "Look! He is coming with the clouds . . ." The unveiling (or revealing) of Jesus Christ as king over the earth is the overarching theme of John's prophecy. This awe-inspiring revelation of the returning king has enormous implications and consequences—no wonder it takes John twenty-two chapters to describe the prequels and sequels of these momentous events! Here's what else you discover in the opening:

- This book is a prophecy (1:3) revealing the person and plan of Jesus Christ (1:1). The introduction functions somewhat like a movie preview.

- There is a blessing for those who read and put this prophecy into practice (1:3).

- The author of the prophecy is a man named John (1:4).

- The intended readers are the seven churches of Asia (what we call Asia Minor) (1:4).

These churches were located in what is today Western Turkey.

- This prophecy was written on the island of Patmos (1:9), belonging to Greece today, and lying some thirty-seven miles off the coast of Western Turkey.

- The prophecy began with a vision of the risen Christ, which occurred on a Sunday. This is the meaning of the expression "the Lord's day" (1:10).

What is fascinating about the prologue is the clear sequence indicated for the origin of this document. Notice the following chain of transmission:

$$\boxed{\text{God the Father}} \rightarrow \boxed{\text{Jesus Christ}} \rightarrow \boxed{\text{angel}} \rightarrow \boxed{\text{John}} \rightarrow \boxed{\text{Seven Churches of Asia}}$$

Though written in the first century AD, this book continues to encourage and challenge readers of any time and place to hold on to faith in Christ no matter how great the cost. Revelation concludes with a general warning against tampering with its contents (22:18). This assumes that later readers will indeed read it. The primary point of the sequence of transmission is simply this: the content isn't just made up by some individual, however well-intentioned or in tune with the spiritual vibes he may have been; it comes from God the Father. If John cared so deeply about preserving the words of Revelation, then it shares a message that shouldn't be ignored!

OPENING VISION: ENCOUNTER WITH CHRIST (REVELATION 1:9–20)

A vision of the risen Christ serves as the centerpiece of chapter 1. The vision is described using symbols that are explained for the reader. There can be no doubt who the person is: "Son of Man" is a favorite title Jesus used for himself during his earthly ministry.

The Son of Man John sees wears a garment like a high priest and is depicted with the attributes of God the Father in the Old Testament: head and hair like white wool, eyes like a flame of fire, feet like burnished bronze, and a voice like the sound of many waters (See Dan 7:9–10; 10:5–6; Pss 29:3; 94:4; Ezek 1:24; 43:2). The point of the imagery is clear: John believes Jesus Christ is truly divine and functions like a priest. In fact, we will discover something stunning about the kind of priestly ministry Jesus has already performed when we look at chapters 4 and 5.

> Son of Man: See the Gospels Matthew, Mark, Luke and John for the many references to this important title (e.g., Mt 8:20; 9:6; 11:19, 27; 12:8, 40; 13:41; 16:13, 16, 27–28; 19:28; 24:27–44).

Furthermore, and this is especially relevant for John and his congregations on the mainland, Jesus Christ is alive and well! "See, I am alive forever and ever; and I have the keys of Death and of Hades" (1:18). Believers in

Jesus may rest assured: not even death itself can separate a believer from the risen Lord (see Rom 8:35–39). This is just what the believers on the mainland of Asia needed to hear, and it's the same message believers in any time and place need to hear. Courage springs from conviction anchored in a risen Savior who has conquered death and stands with us in our darkest moments.

AN OUTLINE OF THE BOOK OF REVELATION

Verse 19 is important because it broadly sketches the contents of the entire book. John is commissioned to write down three main categories of information conveyed to him by an angel sent by God the Father and the Lord Jesus Christ. Here is the essence of what John writes:

- The vision he has just received of the glorious risen Jesus Christ: "what you have seen" (Rev 1)
- A series of visions depicting the circumstances of the seven churches of Asia: "what is" (Rev 2–3)
- A series of visions portraying the course of events climaxing in the return of Jesus Christ and the creation of a new heaven and new earth: "what is to take place after this" (Rev 4–22)

With this as a brief overview, it's now time to take a peek at what was happening in the seven churches.

SECTION 2

Perseverance

Chapter 3

Good News for the Weary

THE POUNDING ON HIS door in the middle of the night startled Philip from his sleep. His heart thumped in his chest and chills ran up his spine. The Romans had been rounding up Christians at all hours, and he feared his gathering had been found out. Stumbling through the dark toward the door, his legs weak, Philip thought of the families with young children in his gathering. Were they on their way to prison right now? Would the children be killed along with their parents?

The banging on the door resumed. Philip's mind raced through the options. Could he try to run out the door? If there were too many of them, perhaps they'd at least make it quick. And yet, he thought of the followers of the Way who had died in the arena. Their silent testimony had moved him many years ago. Would he dare to rob someone else of an opportunity to witness his martyrdom? His hands trembled as he slid the bolt aside.

A dark, massive man stood in the doorway in a Roman soldier's uniform. Philip gasped.

"Well? Are you going to invite me in?" the solider demanded.

"I . . . I . . . thought you were taking me," Philip stammered.

"Ha! I suppose I should have shouted my name. It's Demetrius."

Philip slumped against the door as his old friend bounded in. If Demetrius wasn't quite a Christian, he was certainly a friend with sympathies for the followers of the Way. Apparently several soldiers in Ephesus worshipped both Jesus and the Emperor.

Lighting two lamps at the table and setting a loaf of bread before Demetrius, Philip settled across from him.

"I was thinking about being tossed to the wild beasts just moments ago," Philip began. "Why would you scare me like that?"

"You Christians are so jumpy. It's not like everyone is out to get you. Just some officials here and there," Demetrius said with a wave of his thick hand. "It couldn't be helped. The centurions know that Christians won't serve in the Roman army. I can't be seen here. And besides, I bring news that is far too important to risk being found out."

"Who has been killed now?" Philip asked with a sinking feeling in his gut. Demetrius always knew about the latest arrests and executions. Though Philip had grown quite fond of his friend with inside information, their meetings usually brought a good deal of bad news.

"It's good news this time. There's a letter—a rather long letter at that—for you to pick up."

"A letter to deliver? It's too risky right now. The last thing I need is to carry around handwritten evidence that I'm a follower of the Way."

"It's from the apostle."

"John?"

Demetrius nodded with a mouth full of bread.

Philip thought of the day they shipped John away to exile on Patmos. He'd given the old man up for dead. Could it be a forgery?

"What am I supposed to do?"

"Have you already forgotten how to be a secret messenger?" Demetrius said as he settled back on a cushion, his armor scraping against the stone wall. "The letter arrives tomorrow in the port along with a shipment of wine. Ask the captain for the new wine, and he'll give you two wine sacks. The letter will be hidden in one of them."

"Do I need to actually buy the wine in the other container?" Philip thought of the loaf that Demetrius had eaten—his food supply until his employer paid him at the end of the week.

Demetrius flicked a few coins on the table.

"Consider it my investment in treasure in heaven."

Philip hadn't slept a wink after Demetrius left. He'd planned the next day to the minute. After picking up the letter he would travel from house to house, telling the elders about the letter's arrival and calling for a meeting the following evening. Some in the Ephesian church had parchment and ink, and so he would have to assemble as many copyists as he could find.

It was critical to keep the letter moving from one church to another. He wanted to produce as many copies as possible. It was the only way to ensure that this rare treasure could survive the supervision of the Romans who were both bored and brutal.

On the following afternoon Philip wandered down the hill from the center of town to the port. To his guilty conscience, every soldier and member of the cult of Artemis eyed him with suspicion. His hands became sweaty, and he rubbed the coins in nervous anticipation. He tried to look about the surrounding hills and the ships sailing in, focusing on anything that wasn't armed or hostile toward the followers of Jesus.

He asked around and found the ship with the wine cargo. The captain had a weathered but kind face. His sympathetic eyes told Philip he understood exactly what was at stake. Philip dropped the coins in his hands and set off for home with his wine sacks. He was caught up in congratulating himself for pulling it off so smoothly that he hardly heard the Roman soldier at the port entrance calling him over.

"You with the wine sacks. I told you to stop! Are you deaf and dumb?"

The other soldiers laughed as a red-faced centurion stomped over to him. Philip's heart sank. This was really it. He thought of Demetrius stopping by a friend's home later in the evening to say he'd been sentenced to death.

"What's in your sacks?"

"New wine," Philip replied, standing as straight as he could. He wanted to go bravely.

"Well, let's see how it compares to the vineyards of Rome." He snatched the sack full of wine from Philip's arms. As the towering soldier threw his head back to drink, Philip became aware that the other sack was quite light. He needed to fake carrying something heavy since it was clearly just stuffed with paper.

The solider spat warm wine all over Philip's feet.

"Horrible! I ought to toss you into the gladiator ring. It can't be worse than drinking this slop."

The soldiers at the port entrance laughed and called out at Philip, but he took his sacks of wine and hustled away. His mind began to race about his next moves—hiding the scroll under his bed would be a start. He'd planned on keeping the wine on hand if he needed to bribe a soldier. The wine no longer struck him as an asset.

After hiding the scroll, he needed to alert the elders and copyists that all was ready. There was so much to do. Each passing soldier and government official who eyed him sent a shiver down his spine. As he walked past the enormous temple of Artemis, he ignored the calls from a priestess. Did she recognize him from the past? Would she wonder why he hadn't been to the temple in so long? He quickened his pace and stumbled over a loose rock, landing himself square in the back of a short man with a bushy beard and wide, terrified eyes.

It was Gaius, one of the church elders. He no doubt thought the person crashing into him from behind was a Roman soldier.

"We need to talk," Philip said to Gaius. "Follow me."

Hustling off the central road in Ephesus, Philip climbed a small hill and settled in a secluded alley in a residential area that provided some breathing room from the center of commerce and Roman soldiers.

"I have a letter from the apostle John. It just arrived today."

"Are you sure it's authentic?" asked Gaius, raising an eyebrow.

Philip seethed inside. This wasn't the time for Gaius to have doubts, to be the dissenting voice, always asking questions. Why had he bumped into the elder who was least likely to help out? Why couldn't the man just trust him?

"I assure you, I have good reason to believe this." Philip didn't want to mention his source. He imagined Gauis, cautious and suspicious, would be the last person to welcome information from a Roman soldier.

"May I see the first page of the document?" Gaius stood stroking his beard, breathing heavy through his nostrils.

It was too much for Philip. He heard the rustling of metal and the thumping of marching Roman soldiers along a nearby street. He had to get out of there. Still, he did as Gaius asked, thrusting the scroll into his hand. Checking down the alley, he took note of an escape path. At the very least he could run for it and save his life, leaving Gaius to fend for himself.

Gaius held the scroll up to his face. With his heavy breathing, it sounded as if he was sniffing it. His incessant beard stroking continued. Philip thought of yanking on the beard in order to snap him back into reality. There were real threats all around them. Only three people in Ephesus knew about this letter from John the apostle.

"Good. It looks authentic," said Gaius as he handed the page back to Philip who stuffed it back into his wine sack. "I feared it was another false letter from the Nicolaitans. They've been wrecking the church in Smyrna, teaching that only spiritual truths matter and people can live as they like."

Philip nodded, looking around for the best way escape from Gaius.

"I'll tell the other elders," Gaius said. "I'm sure you need to find someone to copy the letter."

"Oh, um, yes. Thank you." Philip had almost run off without discussing these details. "I'll head straight to Trypho's after I hide it."

"May God protect you," Gaius said as he slapped Philip on the arm and walked off, looking up and down the street as he walked along. Philip wondered if Gaius would make it. He looked so suspicious, how could a Roman soldier not question him?

Later that evening the church of Ephesus gathered in the courtyard of a larger home. Candles and torches surrounded Philip as he sat before the unrolled the letter. He had been given the honor of being the first reader. The elders lined up beside him, each prepared to take a turn reading. Two copyists sat at his feet.

Philip had peeked at the letter, reading a few lines at home. The words of Jesus continued to burn within him. The rebuke that they had lost their love for God and for one another was all too true. They'd thought too much about survival, about making it another day. Glancing at Gaius, who sat stroking his beard with his eyes closed, he thought of getting up to apologize for being so rude to him. Yes, he would get up and confess his wrong. It was the only place to start. Just as he shifted to stand up, he realized someone was speaking to him. The meeting had begun, and he had to start reading.

As Philip and the elders read the letter from John, the people remained silent and still. Everyone knew three ways to escape if the Romans barged into the front door, but the heavenly visions and words of encouragement in this most unusual letter prompted each person to view the terrifying force of the Romans in a different light. Soon they forgot about their escape routes as they rediscovered the power of God.

Gaius, an educated elder who grew up as a teacher in the local synagogue, interrupted at certain points in order to explain certain scenes that resembled stories in the Jewish scriptures.

The world cracked open for Philip in new ways. He understood realities that had been completely beyond him before.

Walking home in the darkness, Philip thought of his Roman friend Demetrius. Demetrius believed to a certain degree, but he wasn't ready to make a commitment to following Jesus. Demetrius still served the antichrist. Thinking of the final judgment, Philip knew what he had to do. Setting off for the Roman barracks, he needed to tell Demetrius about this letter from John. He marched with confidence to the barracks as if he was leading an invading army. The power of God was in him. He sensed the Spirit's presence hovering throughout the world. As he thought of staring the sentry in the eyes, Philip realized he was no longer afraid.

Chapter 4

Seven Ways to Persevere

IN THIS CHAPTER

- The types of persecution Christians in the seven churches faced.
- How Revelation addressed the challenges of the seven churches.
- The wrong kind of perseverance.

THE APOSTLE JOHN WAS greatly concerned that Christians in his day persevere in their faith because of their extreme suffering and the temptation to drop Jesus in order to enjoy an easier life. Clearly, the Holy Spirit intends that Christians of any time and place likewise persevere to the end. If they failed to persevere against the false teachers, the temptation to sin, and the violence of the Romans, they could end up on the outside of the New Jerusalem.

Trusting in Jesus Christ as Savior and Lord in spite of opposition, ridicule, persecution, and suffering of any kind is what perseverance is all about. Sometimes perseverance requires staying focused in the midst of many distractions, but other times it may require significant sacrifices. In short, perseverance means staying the course whatever happens—and a lot of tough things can happen throughout our lives.

In John's day, being a follower of Christ was no easy matter. Unbelieving neighbors ridiculed Christians for belonging to this "new superstition" that was taking root in the Roman province of Asia—a superstition that some Romans viewed as a threat.

> The following section from the Greek historian Tacitus illustrates the hostility of many against the new group called Christians. The context is Tacitus's description of Nero Caesar's cruel massacre of Christians following the fire of Rome in AD 64. "Nero fastened the guilt and inflicted the most exquisite tortures on a class hated for their abominations, called Christians by the populace. Christus, from whom the name had its origin, suffered the extreme penalty during the reign of Tiberius at the hands of one of our procurators, Pontius Pilatus, and a most mischievous superstition thus checked for the moment, again broke out not only in Judaea, the first source of the evil, but even in Rome, where all things hideous and shameful from every part of the world find their centre and become popular." (Tacitus, *Annals* xv. 44. [C. K. Barrett, *The New Testament Background: Selected Documents* (rev. ed.; San Francisco: Harper & Row, 1987) 15–16]. "Christus" is almost certainly a reference to Christ and "a most mischievous superstition" probably alludes to the Christian teaching on the resurrection of Jesus.

The pressure endured by early Christians was of several kinds. It might have been economic, involving the loss of a job or a boycott against one's business. It might have been psychological in terms of ridicule, rejection, and verbal threats. Lastly, it might have even occasionally taken the form of physical abuse, torture, and death. When John wrote to the seven churches of the province of Asia, at least one Christian, named Antipas, had already been martyred in the city of Pergamum because of his faith in Christ (Rev 2:13: ". . . Antipas my witness, my faithful one, who was killed among you, where Satan lives.").

In light of this grim reality, the book of Revelation contains numerous passages addressing this prospect, beginning in the opening chapter where we read these remarkable words from the risen Christ: "Do not be afraid. I am the First and the Last. I am the Living One; I was dead, and now look, I am alive forever and ever! And I hold the keys of death and Hades" (Rev 1:17–18). Believers may rest assured because Christ has overcome death and promises that all who believe in him have already crossed over from death to life and will be resurrected from the grave (John 5:24–29).

But what should a Christian do when pressured and persecuted by unbelieving, hostile neighbors? Is it appropriate to retaliate? Should one respond in kind and heap abuse on those who persecute? Or should one retreat into a shell and seek to withdraw from any social contact? Or should one deny faith in Jesus (at least temporarily) in order to avoid unnecessary persecution and suffering? What is the Christian response to this kind of situation? Revelation provides guidance that assists us in confronting similar circumstances in our own time and place.

PASTORING VIA POST (REVELATION 2–3)

A good starting point for Revelation's message on perseverance is the section dealing with John's seven letters addressed to the seven churches of Asia (Rev 2–3).

The seven letters display similarities to prophetic writings found in the Old Testament prophetic books, especially Amos 1–2. Accordingly, John, also a prophet, addresses each congregation with words of praise and encouragement, warning and rebuke. Several features of these messages deserve comment in order to appreciate what is going on in the book of Revelation and what it has to say about perseverance.

Just like prophetic messages in the Old Testament and the teachings of Jesus (as in the Sermon on the Mount), John organized his material in ways that made it more easily remembered. In a culture where only about fifteen percent of the population was able to read, great emphasis was placed on verbally sharing messages and the ability of the listeners to recall the messages from memory. Not surprisingly, John arranged each message with a regular structure and pattern. Here is the basic structure:

- Command to write: "To the angel of the church in [. . .] write."
- Credentials of the sender: "These are the words of [. . .]"
- Commendation or condemnation of recipients: "I know [. . .]"
- Concern: "Remember, Do not fear, Repent [. . .], etc."
- Call for obedience: "Whoever has ears [. . .]"
- Challenge: "To those who are victorious [. . .]"

Despite the similar structure of each message, each congregation is addressed in light of its own unique circumstances. Of special interest is the fact that the credentials of the risen Christ, drawn from the opening vision (Rev 1:10–18), vary and are custom-made for each house church. Furthermore, the challenge to overcomers in the respective churches is relevant to their particular needs.

It's important to remember that in the first century AD, there were no special buildings called churches. The churches (or assemblies) met in the homes of Christians, usually more well-to-do Christians, who had a house that included an open courtyard and several rooms in which a small number of believers could meet for worship. In fact, it wasn't until the third century AD that buildings called churches actually came into use. Notice that even in the capital city of Rome in the 60s, the apostle Paul refers to "the church that meets at their house" (Rom 16:5; see also 16:14–15).

We've already seen that the risen Christ explained to John the meaning of the seven stars and seven lampstands: the stars are angels linked in some way to each church and the lampstands represent the churches (Rev 1:20). The symbol of a lampstand is especially appropriate for a church since Jesus reminded his disciples: "You are the light of the world. A city on a hill cannot be hidden. Neither do people light a lamp and put it under a bowl. Instead they put it on its stand, and it gives light to everyone in the house. In the same way, let your light shine before others, that they may see your good deeds and glorify your Father in heaven" (Matt 5:14–16). Believers, both individually and corporately, are called to be witnesses by word and deed to the truth of the gospel even in the midst of persecution. Our special interest in these messages centers in what they tell us about perseverance.

Just who in the world are these seven angels? At least four main views have been suggested:

- The angels are the individuals who hand delivered John's messages to the churches, sort of like postmen.

- Perhaps the angels are the pastors of the respective churches.

- Some try to give the word angel the meaning of "spirit" or "attitude."

- What if we simply take John at face value and assume that each church has a guardian angel? After all, there are several passages in the New Testament in which angels assume some role in protection and oversight (Matt 4:6, 11; 18:10: 26:53; Juke 15:10; Acts 5:19; 12:7–15; 27:23). Paul can even speak of angels who take note of what happens during Christian worship services (1 Cor 11:10). We think this explanation best fits the context.

EPHESUS: PERSEVERANCE WITHOUT LOVE

The church at Ephesus was located in the largest city in the entire province of Asia, a city of a quarter million inhabitants. It boasted a panorama of splendid theaters, public baths, market places, a forum (public square where legal and political matters were decided), gymnasiums, luxury villas, and magnificent temples, especially the crown jewel of the city, the Temple of Artemis. This temple, considered one of the seven wonders of the ancient world, measured 420 feet long by 240 feet wide and its ornate roof was held aloft by 117 Corinthian columns 60 feet high. The centerpiece was a gigantic statue of the fertility goddess Artemis (Diana), open to the sky. Silver statues and amulets of her image were sold in large numbers, especially as good luck charms for women who wished to have children, and contributed greatly to the wealth of the city (see Acts 19:23–41).

In this great city, a number of Christian house churches thrived. Founded by Paul in the mid-50s (Acts 19) and later overseen by Timothy, Paul's assistant, in the 60s (1 Tim 1:3), the congregation had weathered some hard times. The risen Christ explicitly commends them for their perseverance and endurance: "I know . . . your perseverance . . . You have persevered and have endured hardships for my name, and have not grown weary" (Rev 2:2–3).

It must have been extremely difficult to be a Christian in Ephesus. As indicated above, the city was famous throughout the Roman world for its great shrine to Artemis and thousands of pilgrims flocked to Ephesus in order to acquire the protection and blessing of this supposed goddess. Christians did not and could not support this cult. The result was that the many people who directly profited from this "religious industry" (temple priests and priestesses, wardens, silversmiths) and the many who were beneficiaries (shopkeepers, souvenir peddlers, innkeepers, etc.) expressed open hostility and contempt for followers of Jesus. Paul nearly found himself right in the middle of a riot over this issue (Acts 19:23–41).

Ephesus was also well-known for its magic and dark arts (Acts 19:19–20). Many so-called gods and goddesses were venerated in Ephesus. Especially characteristic of this era was the practice of "syncretism," in which several religious or philosophical traditions were mixed together to form a new system. Apparently, the Ephesian house churches expelled a number of self-professed Christian apostles who set up shop among the congregations and sought to mix Christianity with other teachings. The Ephesian church is commended for vigilance. Truth matters. Deviation from apostolic teaching is not an option for Christians. Faithfulness to Christ demands keeping the teachings of Christ with integrity and purity.

There is, however, a major problem in Ephesus. They have cooled in their love for others (Rev 2:4–5). Perhaps the sharp conflict with false teachers, the constant rejection by their pagan neighbors, and the oppression by the city fathers and business community spilled over into the church. That is, they returned the hostility and animosity with the same spirit. This is not the way Christianity is to be lived out. Love is the preeminent quality that Christ wants to see reproduced in his followers (1 Cor 13), and Peter reminds his readers that it is commendable to suffer for doing good (1 Pet 2:19–21).

The Ephesians desperately needed to recover that spontaneous love that flows from the heart of one who has encountered the love of God in Christ (Eph 3:17–19; 1 John 4:16–21). We cannot speak of perseverance without continuing to love one another, even our enemies, in spite of their unloving attitudes and actions toward us.

This takes a measure of grace only the Holy Spirit can provide. There is simply no support in the New Testament for returning evil for evil. The opposite must be the case: return good for evil (Rom 12:17–21). If this sounds completely unreasonable—even stupid!—just remember that New Testament Christianity rewrites the rules according to God's standards. Only Christ and his Holy Spirit can transform our attitudes and actions to conform to this seemingly impossible demand to love others (Rom 12:1–2). Do we have ears to hear what the Spirit is saying to us?

SMYRNA: IMPRISONED FOR CHRIST

Some forty miles to the north of Ephesus lay Smyrna (modern Izmir). The city was the first of the Asian cities to be granted the right to build a temple venerating Caesar Augustus as a god. Not surprisingly, the Smyrnean church was experiencing affliction for refusing to worship Caesar (Rev 2:9) and the prospect for some of them was even more frightening: "the devil will put some of you in prison to test you" (Rev 2:10). God's archenemy, the devil, was at work behind the scenes stirring up hostility against the Christians.

It does not take much imagination to figure out why these believers were coming under fire. As Christians they simply could not participate in the public ceremonies that invoked Caesar as Lord and offered up sacrifices to him as a god. The problem was that their neighbors viewed this non-participation as an act of treason against the state. To pagans, the welfare of the city and empire depended on loyal participation in the rituals of emperor worship. Accordingly, they viewed the Christians as enemies of the people and state. Pressure was no doubt placed on the city officials to take action against this dangerous element in their midst and stamp it out before something terrible happened to the city.

Furthermore, it's likely the primary informers against the Christians were Jews living in the city. Jews were the only ethnic-religious group exempted from emperor worship because of their strong commitment to worshipping one God and their ban against all images of the deity (see Exod 20:3–6). In the early days of the Jesus movement, Christians were considered by Roman officials as a group within Judaism and thus also exempt from emperor worship. Apparently, Jewish leaders were complaining to the Roman officials and insisting that only they, not the Christians, were Jews, and that Christians were a foreign, non-permitted religion in the empire ("the slander of those who say they are Jews and are not, but are a synagogue of Satan" [Rev 2:9. See also Acts 18:12–17]).

It appears that in Smyrna, at least, this accusation was accepted and the authorities cracked down on Christians. During the second century AD, the Roman state finally instituted an empire-wide purge of Christians resulting in thousands of Christian martyrs. At the point when the book

Modern readers of this passage about "the synagogue of Satan" must not take this out of context and use it to demean or demonize Jews today. John's language resembles that of the Old Testament prophets who denounced Israel and Judah for their lack of covenant faithfulness. From John's perspective, a Jewish Christian, the true Israel consists of those who put their faith in Jesus of Nazareth as Savior and Lord. Obviously, the Jewish community of Smyrna, for the most part, rejected this claim and opposed the Christians who also claimed to be Jewish. While we may find fault with their hostile actions against the Christians, we can at least appreciate the reason for their antagonism. A truly Christian response to Jews or any other religious group (such as Muslims, Buddhists, or Hindus) is not name-calling or political measures designed to persecute or hinder free religious exercise, but a courteous and respectful acceptance. Only in such an atmosphere of respect and recognition of full humanity can effective evangelism be successful. And when such individuals reject our message about Christ, we must still treat them as neighbors, not enemies: "Love your neighbor as yourself" (Matt 12:31; Rom 13:9; 15:2; Gal 5:14; Jas 2:8).

of Revelation was written (about AD 95), this was not yet the case and persecution was only sporadic and local.

Detention in prison was not, strictly speaking, a form of punishment in the first-century world. It was a holding tank until a verdict was handed down and a sentence carried out. The sentence might amount to caning (being beaten with wooden rods as in Acts 16:22–23), flogging with a whip (see Matt 27:26), being sent to the mines (where one's life expectancy was short) or into slavery, monetary fines, exile, or capital punishment, such as decapitation or, in cases of treason or heinous crimes, crucifixion. However, the period of confinement was no picnic, involving wretched living conditions and often including torture in order to gain more information about others who were suspected.

Jesus' message to the Christians at Smyrna comes down to this: "Be faithful, even to the point of death, and I will give you life as your victor's crown" (Rev 2:10). Are you prepared to follow the Savior down the same road he trod? Being a follower of Christ is serious business. He made this point crystal clear to his disciples: "Whoever wants to be my disciple must deny themselves and take up their cross and follow me. For whoever wants to save their life will lose it, but whoever loses their life for me and for the gospel will save it" (Mark 8:34–35). Christian perseverance begins with a decision to follow Christ through good times and bad. The Christians in Smyrna were not guaranteed smooth sailing or even deliverance from the hard times ahead. Rather, the risen Lord assured them that he knew about the persecution to come and would ultimately save them from the power of sin and death behind the Roman Empire.

PERSEVERING IN PERGAMUM

Seventy miles to the north of Smyrna lay the city of Pergamum, perched atop a hill high above the Caicus River valley. On the summit of the acropolis sat a temple to Zeus with a great altar. Many other temples to various Greek and Roman deities dotted the landscape of Pergamum, not the least of which was a temple in which Caesar was venerated as a god. No wonder the risen Christ refers to Pergamum as the place "where Satan has his throne" (Rev 2:13). And no wonder the believers were under enormous pressure to conform to the Empire's religion. But to their everlasting credit, Christ commends them: "You did not renounce your faith in me, not even in the days of Antipas my faithful witness, who was put to death in your city—where Satan lives" (Rev 2:13). Once again a reminder: commitment to Christ carries consequences, some of which may be life threatening.

Perhaps we may be surprised to see that Jesus does not offer any explanation about why some believers were being martyred. Rather, the promise of Jesus is quite general: he will come and fight against their enemies at some point and give them eternal life. It's assumed that they will hold onto their faith even at the point of death. While that may disturb us today, this exchange between Jesus and his church reminds us that Jesus promised that his disciples may receive similar treatment. If our Lord is executed, should we expect better treatment? The early church developed a strong sense of faithfulness proven through enduring martyrdom. The renowned desert father Antony even put himself in positions where he essentially dared the officials to put him to death. We do not quite have a grid for this kind of thinking today. However, the promise of Jesus never leaving or forsaking his people does not necessarily mean they will be spared suffering or even martyrdom. The promise is that he will bring justice to this earth, put an end to evil, and raise his faithful people to new life. As the people of Pergamum took stock of their situation, we can imagine that they needed encouragement and assurance that their risen Lord would be able to raise them to new life if they laid their lives down. The immediacy of Revelation's message for a suffering church jumps off the pages: Jesus will return to conquer the forces of evil (be that Rome or any other similar power) and raise his people to new life in the peaceful paradise of the New Jerusalem. There is a cost to persevering in the present, but there surely are future rewards on their way.

This is also a good place to remind ourselves that in terms of sheer numbers, there are more martyrs for Christ today than ever before. How often do we pray for our brothers and sisters in Christ who are undergoing a baptism by fire? We need to express our solidarity with them in prayer and, where possible, concrete aid and assistance. May we, too, hear what the Spirit says to the churches and be victorious. Then we, like the faithful at Pergamum, will get "a white stone with a new name written on it, known only to the one who receives it" (Rev 2:17). In the Greco-Roman world, a white stone sometimes served as an admission ticket to athletic contests or theater performances. For the Christian, it symbolizes admission to paradise—far surpassing anything this world can offer! The new name symbolizes a new relationship with God (see Gen 17:5, 15; 32:27–30; Isa 56:2; 62:2 for some Old Testament examples).

THYATIRA: DANCING WITH JEZEBEL

The church at Thyatira is likewise commended for their perseverance and the notable fact that they were "now doing more than [they] did at first" (Rev 2:19). Typically, Christians tend to cool in their enthusiasm and service as time goes by. Not the Thyatiran Christians. In this they serve as admirable role models for all of us.

But there is a serious problem in the house churches of Thyatira. A toxic teaching is poisoning the church. A woman, claiming to be a prophetess, is apparently urging Christians to loosen up their beliefs and practices. Rather than risk rejection and reprisal for refusing to participate in the imperial cult and the trade guild dinners in which sexual immorality was rampant, this woman assured her listeners that participation was okay and carried no divine restrictions. In short, you could have your cake and eat it too!

John makes it clear to the Christians in Thyatira that partial obedience or selective faithfulness is an unacceptable position for followers of

Christ, who endured rejection and death. Just as Jesus warned about a heart divided between God and money, and Paul warned that sexual sin is a sin against your own body (1 Cor 6:18), John draws a clear line in the sand. They are hanging in the balance between receiving God's reward or trusting in "Satan's deep secrets" (Rev 2:24). The prophets railed against the people of Israel in Old Testament times for their attempts to serve the Lord and other so-called gods (1 Kgs 18:21; Isa 1:1–31; Jer 5). It always resulted in spiritual and moral disaster. And yet every generation produces its Nicolaitans, Balaams, and Jezebels who urge believers to take the path of least resistance that undermines the rule of the risen Christ in their lives. If they were not willing to serve Jesus as their Lord in their hour of need, they

One of the significant features of the city of Thyatira was its large number of trade guilds (somewhat like trade unions). These included wool, linen, and leather workers, as well as potters, bakers, bronze-smiths, and even slave dealers. Thyatira was famous for its purple dye made from the murex seashell. Purple garments were sought out by royalty and nobility and fetched a handsome price. You may recall that a woman named Lydia, who lived in Thyatira, was a dealer in this purple cloth. On a business trip to Philippi, she heard Paul preach the gospel and became a Christian (Acts 16:14). Each guild had a patron deity it honored with regular suppers. Besides offering a sacrifice to this deity, these meals became opportunities for sexual immorality (see 1 Cor 5:9; 6:9, 12–19; 10:14–22).

could lose out on the reward that he would bring one day.

It's also possible that this "Jezebel" was teaching that what one did in the body had no effect whatsoever on the spirit. On this view, Christians could worship Caesar and participate in trade guild sacrifices, indulging in the excesses that accompanied them, without doing harm to their spirits. This later became a major plank in the platform of Gnosticism, an early deviation from Christianity that taught matter is evil and the spirit is good. Since spirit was ultimately the only thing real, so the argument went, what one did in the body was no big deal. This runs counter to the clear teaching of Scripture (see 1 Cor 3:16; 6:12–20; Rom 12:1–2; 13:11–14), and the early church fathers sharply condemned this heresy.

This self-professed prophetess is given the symbolic name Jezebel. Jezebel was Ahab's queen in Israel during the days of Elijah the prophet (1 Kgs 18–19). She was a fanatical follower of the immoral fertility cult associated with the Canaanite storm god Baal and his female consort Asherah. Sacred prostitution was practiced as a part of the ritual in order to induce Baal to send rain and fruitful seasons. Once Baalism was introduced into a society, hormones were sufficient to assure its continuance. The practice of this cult by many Hebrews was a major cause of the destruction and exile of both Israel and Judah.

The Christians in Thyatira had two paths before them. On the one hand, they could accept the false teachers among them, indulge in the pagan rituals, and reap the economic benefits of being part of their mainstream society. On the other, they could trust in the promise of Jesus through John: persevere in this time of suffering and they would one day rule with Christ. Perseverance is possible only when one is completely loyal to the one, living and true God (see Exod 20:1–11; Matt 5:8; 6:24; Jas 4:4; 1 John 2:15). Just as God delivered Israel from the seduction of Jezebel, the Holy Spirit is able to deliver us from our desires that fight against God's presence in our lives (Gal 5:16–17).

SLEEPWALKING IN SARDIS

Thirty miles to the south of Thyatira and about fifty miles east of Smyrna on the coast, lay the important transportation and commercial hub of Sardis. Sardis had an almost legendary past, being the capital of the ancient kingdom of Lydia and famous as the city of King Croesus. He amassed so much wealth the saying "as rich as Croesus" became a byword, and the fame of the city was further enhanced as the place where gold and silver coins were first minted. Sardis was a golden city in a golden age.

Another feature of this grand city was its acropolis towering some 1,500 feet above the city. This heavily fortified stronghold was seemingly impregnable and the citizens of Sardis felt quite secure possessing such a refuge in case of attack. The problem was that twice in Sardis' history this false sense of security had proven fatal. Both Alexander the Great and Antiochus III captured the fortress primarily because no watchmen were posted to guard its steep slopes. The Sardians thought no army could scale the cliffs. How wrong they were!

In some respects the church at Sardis is a mirror image of the famous city. One might even say that the believers at Sardis were spiritually sleep-walking. They appeared to be awake but in fact they were dead on their feet. They were headed for spiritual disaster if they didn't wake up. The risen Christ called for immediate action: "Wake up! Strengthen what remains and is about to die, for I have found your deeds unfinished in the sight of my God. Remember, therefore, what you have received and heard: hold it fast, and repent" (Rev 3:2–3). Whatever it meant for them to sleep, at the very least we can see that they were not actively living their faith, as their deeds were considered unfinished. The disciplines of prayer and Scripture reading alongside serving others and testifying to the story of Jesus are all ways to ensure that our faith stays sharp and complete. Without intentional action, other priorities and "idols" will creep in and may overcome our commitment to Christ. This is a real and present danger as attested by the many similar warnings in the New Testament (see for example, Rom 11:22; Gal 6:9; Col 1:23; Heb 2:1–3; 3:12; 6:4–6; 10:26–27; 10:25). The people who slept in the presence of enemy invaders were in danger of sleeping during a spiritual attack. As Revelation continues, John makes it clear that the forces of evil are actively fighting against God's people.

Thankfully, there were "a few people in Sardis" who had not lapsed into a state of spiritual sleep. They remained alert, vigilant, and held on to their faith in Christ and were promised a reward in God's future city, the New Jerusalem. They "will be dressed in white" and Christ "will never blot out their names from the book of life, but will acknowledge their names before [the] Father and his angels" (Rev 3:5). How tragic to go to sleep spiritually and have one's name removed from the register of citizens belonging to the New Jerusalem! Both the apostle Paul and the apostle Peter were likewise concerned about believers going to sleep spiritually: "So then, let us not be like others, who are asleep, but let us be alert and self-controlled . . . putting on faith and love as a breastplate, and the hope of salvation as a helmet" (1 Thess 5:6–8). "Be alert and of sober mind. Your enemy the devil prowls around like a roaring lion looking for someone to devour. Resist him, standing firm in the faith, because you know that your fellow believers throughout the world are undergoing the same kind of sufferings" (1 Pet 5:8–9).

HOLDING ON IN PHILADELPHIA

The church at Philadelphia, like the other churches, was under great pressure. Apparently, the Jewish community, as in Smyrna, was making life miserable for the Christians. In all likelihood, they incited the local civic authorities to crack down on Christians. The result was that the believers there had "little strength" (Rev 3:8). In spite of the difficulties, the Philadelphian Christians held on to the teaching of Jesus and had not disowned him.

Christ promises this church three distinct things: acquittal by the Lord himself (Rev 3:9), protection from a worldwide trial that is coming (Rev 3:10), and a position of honor in the city of God (Rev 3:12). Each of these deserves a further word of explanation.

The Jewish community at Philadelphia probably excluded Jewish Christians from their synagogues. This exclusion was extremely difficult to bear since the synagogue had been the focal point of their lives before their conversion to Christ. To be thrust out and treated as a traitor was traumatic. Furthermore, these Jewish Christians longed for their fellow Jews to acknowledge Jesus as the rightful Messiah of Israel and Savior of the world. Christ reminds them that at the judgment, Christians will be publicly acknowledged as the true people of God, the heirs of Abraham, Isaac, and Jacob. Perseverance requires that a believer be prepared to endure rejection now, even by one's own people and family (see Luke 12:51–53), and to see through the tears the joy of future justification before the throne of God (Rev 22:3–5).

The promise of preservation from the coming trial is a bit more problematic. In light of the rest of the book of Revelation, this "hour of trial" probably refers to the final period of distress and devastation commonly called the "great tribulation" and connected with the coming of Christ at the end of the age. But in what sense are the believers to be kept from the hour of trial? The whole issue of the great tribulation and its relationship to the rapture of the church has generated enormous controversy and debate among Christians. Since we can scarcely avoid discussing the topic, we offer our take on the matter.

> At some point near the end of the first Christian century, the Jewish synagogues inserted an additional prayer to the *Sh'moneh 'Esreh* (the Eighteen Benedictions). The additional prayer, *Benediction* 12, was a curse: "For the renegades let there be no hope, and may the arrogant kingdom soon be rooted out in our days,

and the Nazarenes and the *minim* perish as in a moment and be blotted out from the book of life and with the righteous may they not be inscribed. Blessed art thou, O Lord, who humblest the arrogant."[1] The Nazarenes were Jewish Christians. This benediction essentially banned Christians from the synagogue services.

1. Translation in C. K. Barrett, *The New Testament Background: Selected Documents*, rev. ed. (San Francisco: Harper & Row, 1987) 211.

In our view, the expression "I will also keep you from the hour of trial" does not refer to a supposed rapture or catching up of believers to heaven before the great tribulation comes (often called the "pre-trib rapture"), but rather to divine protection of believers. In the case of the church in Philadelphia, we can assume that relief of some sort came to them during their trials, but the fact that Jesus wrote to them in the midst of difficult times suggests that Christians are not destined to be raptured from future difficulties either. However the great tribulation unfolds, the promise of the risen Christ is to be present with his people and to reward them for persevering.[1]

The bottom line is this: Christians must be prepared to face the wrath of the antichrist (Rev 13:5–10), confident they will not face the much more consequential and devastating wrath of God (Rev 14:6–12; 16:1–21. See also 1 Thess 5:9). We will address this later in the book.

The third promise to the Philadelphian Christians is especially appropriate. In contrast to their precarious situation at Philadelphia, where fellow citizens exclude them from full participation in civic life and where Jewish Christians are virtually banned from the synagogue, believers in Christ are promised an everlasting presence in God's temple and his holy city, the

1. The closest parallel to this passage comes from another one written by John in his gospel where Jesus prays: "My prayer is *not that you take them out of the world* but that you *protect them from* the evil one" (John 17:15 [italics for emphasis]). The original Greek construction is the same in both instances. In the Old Testament we have an interesting illustration of this divine protection in the story of the plagues on Egypt (Exod 7–11). Note that the Israelites were not physically removed from Egypt during these plagues, but divinely protected and sustained during them.

Finally, the book of Revelation itself strongly suggests that Christians are present during these last traumatic days in that they are repeatedly addressed to persevere and hold on to faith in Jesus. They are described as those who "have come out of the great tribulation: they have washed their robes and made them white in the blood of the Lamb" (Rev 7:14), are called "those who keep God's commands and hold fast their testimony about Jesus" (Rev 12:17), "God's people" (Rev 13:10), and those "who keep his commands and remain faithful to Jesus" (Rev 14:12). It's hard to imagine this does not refer to Christians.

New Jerusalem (Rev 3:12). Once again readers of this message must make a choice: short term membership in sin city or long-term residence in the city of God.

The apostle John penned another letter to the Asian churches in which he also presents this stark contrast: "Do not love the world or anything in the world. If you love the world, love for the Father is not in you. For everything in the world—the cravings of sinful people, the lust of their eyes and their boasting about what they have and do—comes not from the Father but from the world. The world and its desires pass away, but whoever does the will of God lives forever" (1 John 2:15–17). Perseverance involves proper priorities.

LAODICEA: DO NOT DRINK THE WATER!

The last church of the seven churches, Laodicea, is a bit of a puzzle. How can a church with so many assets be so seriously out of tune with the head of the church, Jesus Christ? There is no praise for this congregation, only rebuke. Whatever in the world went wrong?

The primary problem at Laodicea appears to be a smug sense of self-sufficiency ("I am rich; I have acquired wealth and do not need a thing"; Rev 3:17a). This is a far cry from the risen Christ's evaluation: "You are wretched, pitiful, poor, blind and naked" (Rev 3:17b). Unfortunately, the prosperity and inflated sense of self-worth of the city is reflected in the house church as well. Famous for its medical school and eye salve, its high quality garment industry, and its profitable banking establishment, Laodicea was proud of the fact that they had rebuilt their fair city without any imperial aid after a devastating earthquake had rocked the area. Self-reliance is commendable in many areas of life; but in spiritual matters, one must never forget what Jesus said: "Truly I tell you, anyone who will not receive the kingdom of God like a little child will never enter it" (Mark 10:15). A child is completely trusting and does not rely on its own abilities. The Laodicean Christians have apparently forgotten that spiritual success is not primarily measured in material, financial terms. Jesus measures their faithfulness according to their trust in God and obedience to his commands.

The spiritual condition of the church is illustrated by a striking feature of the city. They had no reliable water source in the city itself. This necessitated piping in water from nearby Hierapolis. The problem was that the water of Hierapolis came from hot springs of mineral-laden water. Wonderful for taking hot baths, it was lousy for drinking. Nonetheless, it was piped to Laodicea, during which time it cooled down. The combination of lukewarm, terrible-tasting water was a major downside to living in Laodicea.

Christ draws on this local situation to make a telling spiritual point. The Laodicean believers were, spiritually speaking, so unpalatable, he was about to spit them out of his mouth (Rev 3:16). Hot, mineral water is therapeutic; cold, pure water is refreshing; but barely warm, terrible-tasting water makes you want to spit!

The Christians at Laodicea have only one option: they must repent of their spiritual pride and invite Christ to return to his rightful place as the Lord of their lives (Rev 3:19–20). Paradoxically, if they do that, they will receive what they imagined they already possessed: "I will give the right to sit with me on my throne" (Rev 3:21). Perseverance requires an ongoing recognition that in and of ourselves we are "poor in spirit" (Matt 5:3). Failing to depend on God will make us nauseating to God. Only as we rely on Christ can we truly please him and be of use to others.

WHAT WE DIDN'T READ

Before we move on from the seven churches, there is one further matter about how the churches are told to persevere: Is there any indication in the seven messages that persevering Christians are given the green light to retaliate against their oppressors? Are suffering Christians given any options for fighting back? The answer is clear: it simply is not an option. Perseverance is not a matter of "fighting" an enemy. It has far more to do with clinging to the presence and promises of the risen Christ. But what about the rest of the book of Revelation? Does it provide any further guidance on this issue? Stay tuned.

PERSEVERANCE IS NOT AN ACCIDENT

Persevering Christians have a clear allegiance to Christ that protects them from the lures of false teaching, sexual immorality, pressure to deny Christ, or compromises that could pay off financially. Every Christian addressed in Revelation faced difficult, costly challenges. Following Jesus hardly made life easier. If they were going to persevere in order to receive their reward from Christ, they had to make big decisions about how they would spend their days, who they would serve, and what they would lose.

Most Western Christians can only relate to part of the challenges that the seven churches in Asia Minor faced. We know all too well about the challenges of divided loyalties, sexual immorality, and compromising our beliefs out of convenience rather than conviction. However, we're most likely unfamiliar with financial losses or being physically attacked because of our faith. Perhaps it's hard for us to see the challenge of Jesus' words to the churches about perseverance.

In his messages to the churches, Jesus never promises an immediate end to their sufferings. Being a follower of Jesus does not guarantee smooth sailing. In fact, if they were truly committed to him, they'll most likely attract unwanted attention in the midst of a brutal and oppressive Roman Empire. Although Jesus did promise an end to their sufferings, this is a far cry from a promise to remove the entire church from a hostile world. When Jesus says he will never forsake his people, he means that he will not abandon them but terrible things may still come their way.

As we wrestle with the challenge of persevering today, we have both the hope and the challenge of Jesus' message. God will not solve all of our problems or spare us from hardship . . . at least not yet. There will be plenty of questions, disappointments, losses, and struggles to come. The picture of Revelation is not necessarily a world that will get chaotic and violent one day. It already is that way. We live in a world that calls for perseverance, and that quality will only become more necessary in the days to come. In the midst of the evil at work in our world, the call for Jesus' followers is not to wait for an escape pod. The message of Revelation is to patiently endure our trials and to trust our future to God. Jesus sees the trials of his people, and even though he has overcome Satan and his minions, we must wait for his rule to be fully manifested one day.

When that day comes, the reward for those who persevere through temptation, loss, and pain will be beyond measure.

SECTION 3

Judgment and Justice

Chapter 5

Out of Hiding

PRISCILLA ALWAYS HATED THE olive harvest season. Her arms and legs bore the scratches that came from scrambling through the branches in search of every last olive. Her father had always insisted on being as thorough as possible. Before he took up the tentmaking trade, her brother Timothy had always found a way to convince her to scramble up the tree first and do most of the work for him. As Priscilla looked back at the city, she saw something out of the ordinary that took her breath away.

The Roman soldiers were stomping down their street with a number of the church elders in chains. It was happening. They needed to run.

"Papa! The Romans arrested the elders. I can see them coming down our street."

"Are you sure Priscilla?" her father asked.

Her mother dropped her basket of olives and they spilled across the ground.

"Yes, they're coming our way. I'm not sure if they saw us up here on the hill, but it's just what they warned us about."

"We need to head for the hideout," her father said. "We should have enough daylight to make it there."

Priscilla leapt from the tree into her father's arms and the three of them set off running. Once they reached the woods they slowed to a fast-paced walk. The crunching leaves and snapping branches made Priscilla fear the Romans would hear them and come storming toward them at any moment.

"Do you think they're only arresting elders?" her mother asked her father with eyes wide open. "Or is this just the beginning of something larger?"

"I assume just the elders. That was the rumor we discussed at our last meeting."

"Do you think Timothy is in danger?" her mother asked. "Will the Romans just wait at our home and arrest him when he comes home after work today?"

"I can only hope that they're just going after the leaders and will leave the young people alone."

Her mother started to cry, shaking as she stumbled forward. Her father reached out to catch her but he caught his foot on a tree root. The two of them collided, and while her mother caught herself on a tree, her father hit the ground with a thud. He gritted his teeth and reached for his ankle.

"Just what we needed!" he said.

Priscilla reached out to him but then she saw her mother huddled on the ground sobbing into her arms.

"What will happen to Timothy if they can't find you and decide to arrest him instead?" she wailed.

Priscilla knew what she had to do.

"Mother, give me your scarf, I can help."

"How is that going to help anything?" her mother said, looking at Priscilla with her shocked, tear-filled eyes.

"Just trust me," Priscilla said as she removed the scarf from her mother, tucked her hair inside of her tunic, and wrapped the scarf around her head. I'll go back and bring Timothy with me to the cave. I know the way."

"No! Priscilla! You can't," her father shouted. "Do you want to break your mother's heart?"

"I know what I'm doing. I need to hurry if I'm going to make it before dark."

Priscilla took off running.

"Please! Priscilla, come back!" her mother pleaded.

She blocked their shouts from her mind. They didn't know she'd been running everywhere since the elders warned them about the policies of the new Roman governor that could imprison or kill Christians who wouldn't worship the Emperor. Her legs pumped with an easy rhythm now, although she really just needed to get onto the level path of the road. The sun had dipped quite low at this point, and she would need to rush if she had any hope of catching Timothy before leaving the tentmaker's shop.

When she breathlessly stepped into the shop, her heart nearly stopped. A Roman soldier stood before her brother. Was he arrested? Had she been too late? Should she make a run for it?

It was too late, Timothy saw her.

"Oh look, my little sister just came to see me at work." Turning back to the soldier he said, "Don't worry, I'll get back to work early tomorrow morning to get this tent mended for you."

The soldier turned on his heels and walked out of the shop with a speed that took Priscilla by surprise. He never even looked up to notice her. She could breathe easier now. Perhaps only a few soldiers were part of the attack on the church.

"What's on your mind?" Timothy asked. "You look worried about something. Did the soldier scare you?"

"Not that soldier," Priscilla responded. "But there are other soldiers who just arrested the elders. They were coming for Dad, but we spotted them and made a run for it. Mom and Dad are at the hiding place and are expecting us. We need to leave immediately."

Timothy sat down for a moment and let out a deep sigh.

"I honestly didn't think this day would come. I probably know some of those soldiers too. They're my customers. If they decided to crack down on all of the Christians, I'm in trouble."

"Right now Dad is in even bigger trouble. He also twisted his ankle on the way to the hideout. Like I said, we need to get moving."

"Alright, alright," Timothy replied. "Let me clean up a minute and I'll get moving. We should also pick up some bread if there's any left in the market. It could be a long night."

Timothy and Priscilla walked as quickly as they could on the way out of town, hoping they didn't look suspicious as they hurried out of town at that hour with three loaves of bread tucked in a sack. As they continued along the road, they whispered about what would happen next.

"I need to get back to work tomorrow," Timothy said. "I can't risk losing my job. And besides, either way, the soldiers may get mad at me whether I'm a Christian or if I'm late with those tent repairs. The soldiers don't like to be kept waiting."

"But you can always find another job someplace else," Priscilla said. "At least you can live for another day."

"Are Mom and Dad talking about leaving for another town?"

"They didn't have time to talk about much of anything," Priscilla replied. "They were mostly just scared . . ."

A hand around Priscilla's throat cut her off. She felt a knife up against her skin.

"I'll take your bread and your money," demanded the robber.

Timothy held out the bag.

"It's all yours. Don't hurt her," Timothy demanded, his voice wavering. "My parents have already lost three children."

"Shut up and give me your money before I slit her throat. I don't care about your parents!" the man snapped at him.

As Timothy reached for his coins, Priscilla heard a thud, the robber's head snapped forward, and he fell forward on top of her. She scrambled to her feet and saw a slight man slipping the robber's belt off of him and tying it around robber's wrists behind his back.

"Thank you, sir," Timothy said, stone-still in shock.

Priscilla ran to Timothy and hugged him, turning away from the attacker and their rescuer.

"I'm glad one hit with a rock did it," their rescuer said. "I didn't have much of a plan B. I saw him coming and hid behind a tree a little ways off. I've learned a lot about how to spot a robber on these roads lately, and usually hiding works the best."

"I'm grateful that you took a risk to help us," Timothy replied. "My name is Timothy and this is my sister Priscilla."

"My name is Philip."

"Thank you again, Philip."

"Certainly, but I need to ask you: what are two young people doing on a dangerous road like this so late in the day?"

"We had some urgent family matters," Timothy replied. Priscilla was grateful to be with Timothy. He was such a quick thinker under pressure. "I can see that you must be traveling, but you don't have all that much with you."

Philip patted his bag. "I just have the essentials."

As they walked down the road together in the final shades of twilight, Priscilla and Philip walked together as Timothy kept watch from several paces away.

"Have you lost many friends?" Philip asked.

"Until today, there were just a few Christians imprisoned, but I'm afraid we've lost many friends today," she replied. "They arrested every elder except for my father."

"That's terrible. Did you see if they arrested the families too?"

Priscilla rubbed at her eye as the thought she'd been fighting all day finally took shape in her mind. What became of her friends? Would the Romans torture them to force their parents to deny Christ? She'd been thinking only of survival all day. Now the thought of losing her friends tore at her heart.

"I'm sorry I brought that up," Philip said, placing a hand on her shoulder.

"It's just that I don't understand why God would let the Romans do this to us."

"I don't either," Philip replied. "However, I have a letter with me that may help the church in your city."

"How will a letter help?" Priscilla snapped.

"It's a letter from the apostle John."

"Didn't the Romans . . . kill him?" Priscilla asked, hating to think of the Romans killing anyone.

"No, they couldn't kill John," Philip began. "And he wrote us a letter to help us persevere. Priscilla, there's a war going on. Satan is fighting against God's people right now, and he's using the Romans as his weapon. I don't know when God will get his revenge on the Romans for all of the horrible things they've done, but his justice is coming."

"What's in the letter?" Priscilla asked.

"Well, it's kind of strange actually if you're not familiar with this kind of a letter. There are dragons, unusual beasts, and all kinds of images of what's happening in heaven and all around us. God isn't blind to what's happening. He's present among his people as they suffer. I don't know why he's waiting, but he will set things straight someday."

"I wish he'd hurry up," Priscilla said.

"Sometimes I think that too," Philip replied. "But the best I can figure is that God is patient, willing to wait for people to repent. He will reward everyone who stands firm under suffering, but his judgment of those who persecute his people will be quite terrible. I both want God to settle the score and I fear what that judgment will be like for so many."

"I'm not afraid of God's judgment," Priscilla said. "Those Romans have it coming." She rubbed tears from her eyes.

"You will when you read this letter," Philip said with a sigh. "And anyone else in the future who takes the side of evil in persecuting the church will certainly pay for it. We can only pray that they'll repent."

As Priscilla thought of God's judgment of the Romans one day, she felt something squish under her foot. Looking down at the ground, she found little clumps of olives along the road. Was this a sign from her parents? Could they be near the hiding place? It was so hard to tell in the dark.

"Mother?" she called out.

"Priscilla! We're over here," her mother called out.

Mother and daughter ran toward each other and embraced in a clearing just off the woods.

"Who is that with Timothy?" her mother asked.

"This is Philip," Priscilla replied. "He has a message for us from the apostle John."

Chapter 6

God's Justice Will Win

IN THIS CHAPTER

- God's unlikely answer to injustice.
- Does Hell fit into God's future justice in Revelation?
- Where the church will one day find justice.

WHEN WE HEAR ABOUT a friend who is cheated by a contract, a business that harms its employees, or a criminal attacking a neighbor, we long for justice. We pull for justice every time we watch a movie, rooting for the hero trying to set things right. We anticipate resolutions in novels where the main character can make sense of a difficult past and move on. Most of us can probably count on one hand the number of novels or movies where there's no resolution or restoration of justice.

We long to see the wrongs in our world set straight. This desire is hardwired into us and bubbles to the surface in our art and entertainment. It shouldn't surprise us that the writers of Scripture take great pains to let their readers know that God will one day bring justice to our world. The symbols, visions, and prophecies in Revelation all point to a day when every secret will be revealed, everyone will be judged according to their deeds, and God will render a just judgment. Before we imagine ourselves shaking in fear before a white throne, let's step back to remember John's audience and what these images about judgment would have meant to them.

SECTION 3: Judgment and Justice

John's readers lived in a time where God's justice seemed particularly far away. Rome and their pagan neighbors were winning by every measure. Rome controlled the courts, the military, and even religion—at least Rome tried to control who, what, and how people worshipped. John's readers were wondering whether God saw them faithfully holding onto the truth of Christ that had been passed onto them. Would God reward them for resisting sexual temptation, suffering the loss of possessions, caring for the poor and destitute, and even giving up their lives as martyrs? While faced with incredible pressure to give in, count their losses, and yield to the seemingly unsurpassed power of Rome, they needed the comfort of knowing that God's justice would one day win, rewarding the faithful and punishing the persecutors of God's people.

Revelation "reveals" the fallen, chaotic nature of our world with slain saints crying out for justice and terrifying images of beasts and a dragon. There's no doubt that all have sinned and fallen short of the glory of God (Rom 3:23), and some have even gone so far as attacking the people of God in the service of the beast. The seven churches reading Revelation knew firsthand about the fury of the beast. However, we have seen the beast's handiwork in atrocities throughout history and into our present day. There's every reason to expect that Christians will continue to suffer and evil will continue to be manifested as the poor and defenseless are exploited and attacked until the return of Christ. John presents a series of symbols and visions that offer us clues about how the beast will one day be destroyed once and for all and God's justice will be completely restored to our world at the end of the age.

In Revelation 20:11–15 we read about a great white throne on which God sits in judgment. He has two books: a book of life and a great set of books that record everything a person has done: both the good and the bad. As the Psalmist says, "You have searched me, LORD, and you know me. You know when I sit and when I rise; you perceive my thoughts from afar. You discern my going out and my lying down; you are familiar with all my ways" (Ps 139:1–3). The book of Revelation agrees. Jesus possesses exhaustive knowledge: he "knows" everything about the seven churches (Rev 2:2, 9, 13, 10; 3:1, 8, 15) and, like God the Father, "will give to everyone according to what they have done" (Rev 22:12). He can do this because he too is "the Alpha and the Omega, the First and the Last, the Beginning and the End" (Rev 22:13).

48

For the first readers of Revelation, this all-knowing God on the throne is a reminder to persevere in their faith and even an encouragement that God is more than able to give them the reward they deserve. God had also seen all of the ways the Romans, their pagan neighbors, and the false teachers in the church who had conspired against them. God had seen the suffering of the seven churches as the power of Rome brought suffering and injustice. The slaughtered Lamb, the rider on the white horse, and the figure seated on the white throne offered different angles of the same truth: God has overcome the powerful forces in this world and the evil powers animating them.

The images of the final judgment were not necessarily meant to strike fear into already beleaguered Christians—with the exception being those captivated by false teaching or tempted to abandon Christ. The final judgment of God is a time for God's people to finally step into the light without fear before a just and impartial judge who would render true justice and who had the power to carry it out. Both the holy devotion and the obedient acts of the church will one day be rewarded.

In striking contrast to the bloody *Pax Romana* that had brought Rome's version of peace to the world by conquering Rome's enemies, God will judge people of all nations according to righteous standards. In addition, God's path to peace and justice was achieved not through conquest but through the suffering and death of Christ. As the Romans brutally guarded their power, the seven churches were encouraged to entrust themselves to God's judgment and to endure persecution and even death much like the Son of God. The cross wasn't just the path to salvation from sin. The way of the cross—the way of suffering—was also the way to overcome the evil of their age.

HOW THE SLAIN LAMB GIVES JUSTICE

In order to understand how God has answered this long-standing problem of injustice in our world, we return to the fifth chapter of Revelation, in which a crisis of major proportions arises in the throne room: no one can be found worthy to open the scroll. John is distraught ("I wept and wept" Rev 5:4). If the scroll is not unrolled, the heirs can't be identified nor can they inherit what is rightfully theirs. This dilemma, however, is only apparent, not real. There is someone who is worthy and able to unroll the scroll.

What follows is a masterpiece of paradox. One of the twenty-four elders assures John that indeed there is a person who can open the scroll of destiny: that person is none other than the Lion of the tribe of Judah, the Root of David, who has triumphed over all God's enemies (Rev 5:5). Both of these descriptive titles were applied to the long-expected Messiah of Jewish tradition growing out of the Old Testament (See Gen 49:9–10; Isa 11:1–9; Jer 23:5; Zech 3:8) and applied to Jesus by the early Christians. The Jewish people longed for a great warrior-king who would punish Israel's enemies, restore them to their place of preeminence, and begin an everlasting reign of peace and righteousness (Isa 9:6–7; 11:1–16). The conquering Messiah would finally bring the justice they craved after suffering under a succession of brutal kings who ruled through fear and brute force. Instead of a conquering warrior dressed in armor like a Roman soldier, there appeared the complete opposite: "a Lamb, looking as if it had been slain, standing in the center before the throne, encircled by the four living creatures and the elders" (Rev 5:6). What's going on?

John is drawing deeply from Old Testament symbolism. Each year at Passover, observant Jews sacrificed a lamb without blemish and the entire family consumed the sacrifice (Exod 12). The lamb symbolized God's gracious "passing over" the Jewish people in Egypt and their protection from God's wrath. They were rescued and delivered from bondage in Egypt and sent on their way to the Promised Land. The lamb died in their place and they lived as a result of his death. In fact, if we can keep the story of the Exodus in mind for future chapters, the images of plagues and "bowls of wrath" will make a great deal of sense as God works to deliver his people from the oppression of Rome while ultimately saving them from their sins and the powers of evil in our world.

The phrase "looking as if it had been slain" shows that the Lamb's throat had been slit. This was the required way to kill animals in Jewish tradition. The blood was drained out and not eaten because it was the means whereby sins were covered. The blood of sacrificial animals was poured out at the base of the altar and completely consumed by the fire—a striking image of sins being totally purged and thus forgiven (Lev 7:26–27; 17:11–12 cf. Ps 103:12).

In the New Testament, we have a remarkable development of Passover and the "blood of the Lamb." According to the Protestant interpretation of the Lord's Supper, one eats Jesus' body and drinks Jesus' blood symbolically during the Lord's Supper, a powerful demonstration of the union of Christ with all those who believe in him (John 6:53–59) and a sharing of his body and blood (1 Cor 10:16–17). In the Roman Catholic and Eastern Orthodox traditions, believers eat the actual "body, blood and divinity of Jesus" when they partake of the consecrated Host (the wafer used in the Eucharist).

In like manner, Jesus Christ died the sinner's death. He bore our sins on the cross and by his act of self-giving love set his people free (John 1:29–36; 1 Pet 1:18–21; 3:18). This is the glory of the cross and is nowhere more powerfully illustrated than in this dramatic scene before the throne of God. No wonder the angelic beings surrounding the throne break out in hymn and joyous praise: "You are worthy to take the scroll and to open its seals, because you were slain, and with your blood you purchased for God members of every tribe and language and people and nation. You have made them to be a kingdom of priests to serve our God, and they will reign on the earth" (Rev 5:9). Rather than waging war against the forces of evil on their own terms in order to bring God's justice, the Lamb has overcome all through his sacrifice and commissioned an "army" of priests. However, the seven churches were not just saved by the Lamb's death, they were also called to suffer like the Lamb and to intercede for their oppressors. They were expected to trust in God's power to overcome both their sins and the forces in the world.

The apostle John highlights the significance of the cross in his gospel by means of escalating anticipation. Very early in this gospel we have Jesus telling his mother "My hour has not yet come" (John 2:4). This "hour" is linked with a revelation of his glory. We are twice reminded of this fact (John 7:6–8; 8:20). Then, suddenly, during the last week of Jesus' earthly life, during the Passover festival in Jerusalem (notice the significance of Passover in all this), he suddenly announces, "The hour has come for the Son of Man to be glorified" (John 12:23). And what is this hour of glorification?

It is the most unexpected moment imaginable, the paradox above all paradoxes. It is when Jesus dies on a Roman cross! "Now is the time for judgment on this world; now the prince of this world will be driven out. And I, when I am lifted up from the earth, will draw all people to myself" (John 12:31–32; cf. 19:16–37). And those who are drawn to the foot of the cross and surrender their lives to the savior are promised that they will share in his glory around the throne: "Father, I want those you have given me to be with me where I am, and to see my glory, the glory you have given me because you have loved me before the creation of the world" (John 17:24).

The Lamb who was slain in an unjust act by the Roman authorities holds the key to justice for God's people and the inheritance of God's people who trust in him. In an epic meeting of symbols, the cross that symbolized justice for the Romans was defeated by the slain lamb that symbolized justice and salvation for John's Christian readers. The Lamb has ensured that the church will receive justice in God's presence one day.

WHEN JUSTICE IS SERVED

The arrival of God's justice was unmistakably good news for the seven churches who were suffering persecution and death. Revelation provides the best news possible for the suffering churches: "There will be no more death or mourning or crying or pain, for the old order of things has passed away. He who was seated on the throne said, 'I am making everything new!'" (Rev 21:4–5). For those who have struggled and suffered in an unjust world tainted by evil, judgment is the dawn of a new, peaceful reality.

However, the justice of God is also a sobering reality for those opposing or persecuting God's people. God must bring justice to the pervasive evil in the cosmos. Anyone opposed to the holiness and justice of God will be shut out of God's New Jerusalem. "Nothing impure will ever enter it, nor will anyone who does what is shameful or deceitful, but only those whose names are written in the Lamb's book of life" (Rev 21:27; cf. 22:15). With the good news of God's justice, we are left with the unavoidable reality of justice that brings punishment to those who attack God's people and oppose his renewed order for the world.

Even the seven churches are warned about the perils of neglecting God's salvation. The risen Christ reminds the church at Thyatira, "I will repay each of you according to your deeds" (Rev 2:23) and the bowls of God's wrath poured out on the earth are not without just cause: "You are just in these judgments, you who are and who were, the Holy One, because you have so judged; for they have shed the blood of your people and your prophets, and you have given them blood to drink as they deserve" (Rev 16:5–6).

In chapter 18, when the final world government at last falls, we learn the ultimate reason: "for her sins are piled up to heaven, and God has remembered her crimes. Give back to her as she has given" (Rev 18:5–6). The scene of final judgment, the great white throne, underscores the fairness and impartiality of God's judgment: "The dead were judged according to what they had done as recorded in the books" (Rev 20:12). With God, who dispenses true justice, the punishment always fits the crime, something that, tragically, is not always the case with human justice.

THE PERPLEXING PASSAGES ABOUT HELL

Those who reject the ways of God are left with the frightening possibility of Hell—the place where God desires no one should end up (2 Pet 3:9). While Revelation does not provide a comprehensive picture of Hell on its own, it provides a number of images that make it a particularly relevant topic as we discuss the justice of God.

A helpful starting point is to define what we mean by the term Hell. A quick search in a concordance shows that the word does not even occur in the various English translations of the book of Revelation. Rather, we have expressions like "the great day of their [God and the Lamb] wrath" (6:17), "your wrath" (11:18), "hour of his judgment" (14:7; cf. 16:5, 7), "wine of God's fury" (14:10), "God's wrath" (15:1; 16:1), and "the great day of God Almighty" (16:14). These all refer, however, to the final moment of God's judgment upon human civilization opposed to him rather than to the final state of rebels. These historical judgments are depicted in the series of trumpet and bowl judgments, all of which occur near the very end of human history.

There are also two provocative references to the Abyss in Revelation, a kind of bottomless pit, from which demonic spirits under the authority of an angel called "the Destroyer" come (Rev 9:11), and from which the beast or antichrist arises (Rev 11:7), and to which Satan is consigned for a thousand years when the Lord Jesus returns in glory (Rev 20:2). But if the Abyss is a kind of demonic detention center, it is still not the place of final punishment.

Instead of Hell, Revelation speaks of a place called "the fiery lake of burning sulfur" (19:20), also described as a condition called "the second death" (20:6; cf. 2:11). After the millennial reign and Satan's release and final rebellion (20:7–10), he, along with death, hades, and "all whose names were not found written in the book of life," were cast into the lake of fire (20:14).

This dramatic image of fire bears a resemblance to references to Hell in the Gospels. Jesus himself speaks more of this horrible place than he does of paradise or heaven. In Matt 5:22, he warns his listeners of "hell fire" (KJV) or "fire of hell" (NIV). He later describes it as a place of both fire and of darkness where there is "weeping and gnashing of teeth" (Matt 25:30). "Fire of hell" is actually a place name referring to the Hinnom valley that surrounds the old city of Jerusalem on the western and southern sides (Josh 15:8; 18:16). It was an infamous place, where human sacrifices were offered to foreign gods (Jer 7:31–34). In fact, Ahaz and Manasseh, two of the worst kings of Judah, sacrificed their children in the fire on an altar called Topheth in this very valley (1 Kgs 16:3; 2 Chr 33:6). It was a kind of Faustian bargain in which the kings sought to demonstrate their loyalty to these false gods by giving their own children in return for material blessings and prosperity for themselves and their country, an act betraying complete abandonment of the one, true, and living God.

Because of these abominations, Jeremiah prophesied that the Hinnom Valley would become the scene of a mass burial (Jer 7:30–34). This came to pass during the siege of Jerusalem by the Babylonians (ca. 587–586 BC). So many people died of famine and disease inside the city, their corpses were drug out, dumped, and burned in the valley in order to prevent the spread of further disease. This gruesome scene of burning corpses thus provided a terrifying image of final punishment. Isaiah the prophet describes a similar scene: "their worm will not die, nor will their fire be quenched, and they will be loathsome to the whole human race" (Isa 66:24) Jesus takes up this imagery (Mark 9:43–49) and he is followed by the apostles (2 Thess 1:7–9; Heb 12:29; Jude 23). During the Middle Ages (especially in the writings of

The Greek term is *geenna* (transliterated into English as Gehenna) and is the Greek translation of the Hebrew *ge hinnom*, ("valley of Hinnom") or *ge ben hinnom*, ("valley of the son of Hinnom)." In other words, this valley was the ancestral inheritance of a certain Hinnom family. Somewhere in this valley, not far from the location of the Jerusalem University College on Mount Zion, Ahaz and Manasseh, and apparently other Judeans, performed these heinous sacrifices. As punishment for these horrible crimes, the Lord decreed that the area would become a mass grave, which over time became a horrifying image of the "second death."

Dante) graphic depictions of Hell took on even more ghoulish features and these have contributed to our modern, nightmarish notions about this place.

We are left with a number of questions at this point. What kind of punishment do the rebellious receive? Is death a place of literal darkness where literal "fire" is impossible? Is it possible to be aware of one's punishment in Hell or is the second death annihilation? Why does Revelation mention people living outside of the New Jerusalem (21:27; 22:15) if those who reject God are supposedly in the lake of fire? We are no doubt dealing with powerful imagery in many of the passages related to Hell, and so we should tread carefully. The consensus of the church has been the view that the punishment given in Hell is everlasting; however, much of this relies on how we interpret passages that may carry symbolic overtones.

For instance, Revelation 20:15 even tells us that death itself will be cast into the lake of fire. One may reasonably ask how is it possible to endure everlasting death if death itself has been destroyed. Whether you side with the majority view that Hell is everlasting or the minority view that God annihilates those who reject him, Revelation may muddy the waters more than would prefer. We can all agree, nevertheless, that separation from God is a tragedy that we desire it for no one. The extent of that separation is where the bulk of the debate takes place.

At the most basic level, Revelation shows us that humanity is destined to stand before God and they will be judged based on whether their life reflected what they professed—a common point with Matthew 25. Those who have chosen their own way over God's will face a separation from God, which we could argue is essentially a continuation of how they have lived their lives while on earth. At the judgment seat, every person who distorted the gospel, violently attacked God's people, or served gods or things other than the one true God will receive a just sentence for the choices they have made. It is fitting that God's justice essentially honors a person's choice—those who have chosen to live without God will also die without God.

What happens next is where we encounter all of our questions about the details regarding Hell. In our view, the imagery of fire and darkness is better interpreted figuratively. That is, since fire produces both destruction and pain, it serves as a powerful metaphor for the folly of rejecting God's offer of forgiveness and trying to go it alone without him. Darkness is a primal, human fear and speaks of being totally isolated and lost. Consequently, many theologians are content to speak of Hell as essentially separation from God and with this we agree. If one chooses to live without God,

God honors that choice. But life without God is separate from his peace and detached from all intimacy with him, like living in solitary confinement. Because God granted us free will when he made us, he allows us to choose. It's hard to understand, but many apparently make that catastrophic choice. Their deeds separate them from a loving Father and as a consequence they live apart from him forever.

WHEN WE STAND BEFORE GOD

Perhaps we would rather skip over these passages that deal with Hell and the justice of God. We don't want to read about anyone being separated from God because we hope that everyone will have a chance to repent and change their ways. Even when we see a villain receive justice in a movie, we hope he'll at least see the error of his ways and experience remorse. As many Western readers encounter the message of Revelation, we are particularly far from suffering and injustice, and therefore it's hard for us to relate to the tensions experienced by Revelation's original audience.

As the churches in Asia Minor waited for deliverance from their oppressors, the thought of God's justice was not a theoretical theological concept. They saw grave acts of evil all around them, and therefore the thought of a just God who is able to punish evil spoke with particular power to their situation. We can perhaps relate to them if we can imagine that God will one day do away with genocide, hunger, slavery, and oppression. We see stories in the news about war and poverty, and as these people, our neighbors, cry out for justice, we can join them in anticipating a future where true justice will be given to all. As God prepares a place where every tear will be wiped away, it's only reasonable to think that those who reject his peace, justice, and healing will have no part among his people. Those committed to their own agendas or those who are violent or abusive have no place among God's future people.

The idea of standing before God's judgment throne understandably strikes many of us as frightening. However, the churches in cities of Asia Minor and those who follow Jesus today can take a very different perspective on this moment. The throne of God is where we will be declared holy and righteous before God because of Christ. This won't be a fearful ordeal where we'll have to plead our case in a courtroom. The Spirit of God assures us that our sins have been forgiven and that God's justice for us will be the reward that Jesus promised his disciples who sacrificed much to follow him. If our lives have been changed by the Spirit of God and we reflect his justice today, we can join the Christians in the seven churches who anticipated a day when God would declare them righteous.

Just as God's people have the hope that they will stand flawless before God because of the Lamb who was slain, they will also enjoy the hope that God's justice will eradicate all forms of injustice. Revelation shows us that God's ultimate plan is to heal the nations and to give peace to his people, but his justice will not make exceptions. We serve a just God who sees our inner motivations and will judge us rightly.

SECTION 4

The Battle between Good and Evil

Chapter 7

Setting Captives Free

ALL DAY THE HUMMING echoed off the dark, cold prison walls. The near but unseen prisoner had arrived a few days ago, and he only stopped humming for meals, sleep, and a guard's punch. As guards dumped a daily meal into each cell, chains rattled and prisoners hissed curses—everyone, except for "the hummer."

What could he possibly be humming all of the time? In fact, the mystery of the humming provided Demetrius with a welcome distraction from obsessing over his life's unfortunate turn. He had spent the past week reviewing the details of his crime. The man had questioned his honesty in the market, and somehow his anger had taken over. A small argument that turned into a violent struggle and left a man dead. The humming interrupted him again. It always did. Perhaps that's why the man hummed all day. He too needed to escape the dark stench of prison, and humming sure beat thinking over the past.

Of course humming wasn't the only thing he heard in the prison. The other prisoners, who came in and out daily often shouted at the humming man.

"You crazy fool, you won't be humming when the Romans crucify you!"

Crucifixion: the word gave Demetrius chills. His case wasn't looking good. Murderers were not shown mercy, especially when they had killed prominent citizens. Why didn't he just let that arrogant old man walk away? What did the pompous bastard expect an honest merchant to do when accused of lying? Could a man just turn away after someone spit in his eye? The murder was an accident. Anyone could see it was just one punch.

The humming grew louder, drowning out the image in Demetrius' mind of the old man crumbling to the ground and a crowd gathering around to seize him.

Wasn't the hummer tormented by guilt or regret? Didn't he have a family to worry about? Didn't he fear death?

The stomp of boots woke him. It was unusually early for the guards to stop by the cells. It wasn't mealtime. The sun had hardly risen. There must be news, and in here, news was rarely good.

"Demetrius!" the guard barked through the bars. "You'll be sentenced today. We're going to miss your smiling face around here."

Sentenced—the word left him cold and searching for words. He had no bravado left. He had no hope. No one had found a way to pardon him or to convince the judge that it had been an accident. There was no explaining away a clear-cut murder, especially when committed by a foreign merchant without Roman citizenship.

He began to weep, his chest heaved and his chains rattled as he lost control of his body, shaking and clutching at his arms to try to steady himself as the guard walked away.

"Friend, can I pray for you?"

The voice was a new one, soft and friendly. He'd never heard it before amidst the chaos and tumult of the prison. The voice lacked the harsh tones of everyone else in the prison. As he took it in, he realized there was no humming.

"What good will prayer do now? I'm a murderer? Save your breath." He meant that. He knew he was beyond hope. And yet, he wanted someone to pray for him. He wanted to talk to someone. The extent of his loneliness finally hit. He'd been alone for weeks in prison while the corrupt legal system exchanged favors and bribes before ruling on his case. At his lowest moment, he needed to speak to someone, even the odd man who hummed all day.

"I know you don't have any hope. I would feel the same way. All the same, I'd still like to pray for you."

"What god would honor a prayer for a murderer?"

"My God will help a murderer who confesses his crime. That includes you. Don't you know that Jesus forgave a murderer who confessed his crime?"

Demetrius should have known. There hadn't been too many Christian's arrested in his city, but some officials still accused Christians of cannibalism or witchcraft when they needed to discredit or rob a Christian. There's no doubt that the man was an oddity, but Christians were never dangerous people. This man most likely had more reason than most to gripe and complain. How could he spend his time humming?

"Don't you worry that your God has abandoned you? Why else are you in chains? Why would your God help me if he's not helping you?" Demetrius replied.

"These chains aren't the end of the story. God isn't done with me, with you, or with anyone else for that matter. I may not see justice in this life, but God will see that justice is done. I just need to patiently wait whether my future is good or bad."

"What makes you so sure?"

"I'm not sure in a way that I can prove to you." The man paused, as if to weigh each word carefully. "It's more of a promise that God has given us. Jesus will return to rid this world of evil and to set everything right. When Jesus is judge, he'll give us what we deserve according to our deeds."

"That's what I'm afraid of!" shouted a man in the next cell over.

"You know," said Demetrius, "I didn't mean to kill a man. I was just angry because he'd called me a liar. Do you mean to tell me that Jesus wouldn't punish me as a murderer?"

"I don't know what you are guilty of, but Jesus will surely be far more merciful than the Romans. And whether or not you meant to kill that man, God forgives those who turn away from their sins and turn to him. Are you willing to repent of what you did?"

"I've been repenting since I ended up in here, but what difference does that make? Isn't that man still dead? I'm still destined to die! What good would Jesus do if I told him I was sorry?"

"I understand that you're afraid," the man said. The words hung in the air. Demetrius would have never admitted out loud that he was afraid. He'd rather die than admit it. In fact, he was about to die, so that was that. And yet, the man cut through all of his questions and despair to speak to the heart of the matter: Demetrius was deeply afraid of the future.

"If I could just pray for you, it may make a difference," the man continued. "I know you don't believe in any of this, but it's not going to make things worse."

"Fine," Demetrius replied, letting out a sigh that sounded more exasperated than he actually felt. He wanted to let the other inmates know that he wasn't falling for this Christian's superstition, even if he wanted the Christian to keep talking until the guards returned.

Before he realized it, the Christian had started praying. The prayer was casual, almost irreverent. Demetrius almost asked if the Christian was talking to him or to God, but then the man started to praise God as the Lord of this world, the conqueror of evil, and the only just judge. He praised God for his love and mercy. He thanked God for the safety of his family, and then he began to mention "brother Demetrius." It was odd, but Demetrius decided to stop asking questions and to wait and see if anything happened.

The Christian spoke of God's mercy, and he mentioned that God knew Demetrius was afraid. He asked God to bring peace and comfort and to even spare Demetrius from his fate. Demetrius let the words sink in and his mind became still.

Footsteps once again echoed throughout the prison. The guards were on their morning rounds to deliver breakfast. The Christian cut off his prayer abruptly, switching back to his humming.

"On your feet!" a guard shouted. Chains rattled and the humming stopped as the Christian gasped for breath.

"That's one last reminder of what we can do to you. You're free to go now. Somebody's watching out for you. The judge threw out your case. But don't worry, they'll be keeping a close eye on you. I'm sure we'll see you again soon."

"Thank you," the Christian replied in a whisper. It could have been in reply to the guard, a defiant kindness that exposed the guard's brutality. But Demetrius heard a two-word prayer of thanks to his God.

The Christian exited into the bright sunrise with a brief shuffling of feet. Demetrius had lost his only comfort in prison. Waiting for his breakfast, he heard the guards moving from cell to cell while the inmates hurled familiar curses and profanities. As he thought of the justice of God, he felt something slip away. His anger at the Romans faded. Even they would have to give an account of their deeds to God one day. Perhaps they were to be pitied most.

"And you," the guard sneered. "You won't need any breakfast. I'll be back for you soon. We're going to take a little walk."

Demetrius' heart sank. This was it. Was there any hope now? Just as he began to second-guess the Christian's prayer, Demetrius felt a presence near him. He still felt afraid. He still dreaded the return of the soldier. But something had changed.

He wasn't alone. Someone knew who he was and just how deeply he regretted his actions. Before he realized what was happening, Demetrius started to hum.

Chapter 8

The Battle between Good and Evil

IN THIS CHAPTER

- The battle between the dragon and the woman.
- Satan's strategies for opposing the people of God.
- How God's people resist evil.

SMYRNA WAS NOT JUST a city ruled by Rome. The citizens of this Roman colony fell over themselves to please the Roman emperors by building temples in their honor and even going so far as building a temple in honor of the Roman Senate. Back in ancient times one of the best ways to lobby politicians was to build them a temple worshipping them as gods.

With so much effort invested in staying in Rome's good graces, we shouldn't be surprised to read that the Christians in Smyrna were particularly hard-pressed because they refused to bow before Caesar. Even worse, the Jewish people living in exile under Roman rule lived in fear of losing their exemption from worshipping Caesar. By the time the Christians started increasing in Smyrna, there was little room for a new religious group who resisted the Roman requirement to bow before Caesar—the very thing that could threaten the special status enjoyed by the Jewish people under

Rome's rule. It is no surprise that John wrote to this church among the others because they were suffering a particularly difficult time of persecution.

If any group of Christians was experiencing the battle between good and evil first hand, it was the church in Smyrna where death and imprisonment were quite possible in an intensely patriotic city for the rule of Rome. The last thing the citizens of Smyrna wanted was a band of political rebels undoing their years of Roman patronage. The choice between Jesus and the worship of Caesar was particularly stark for the Christians in Smyrna. They needed reassurance that God was still powerful and that he was fighting against the cruelty of Rome. As Revelation pulls back the curtain on the spiritual realities behind what we can see, God emerges as powerful and fully engaged in the battle between good and evil.

IS GOD REALLY IN CONTROL?

We may imagine the Christians in Asia Minor wrestling with how to reconcile John's revelation of God's power in spite of their suffering and uncertain circumstances. This brings up the age-old dilemma between human free will and the sovereignty of God. While Revelation does not exactly offer us easy answers, one of the resolutions put forward is that while humans can choose to resist God and to even persecute his people, God will have the last word. In addition, everyone who endures suffering in this life for the sake of Christ will be rewarded in the next life. The scenes that unfold in Revelation spoke to the churches in Asia Minor, offering them comfort and hope. If Paul wrote about the battle between good in evil in his own heart in Romans 7, Revelation paints a picture of the global battle between good and evil.

In the 1979 movie *Apocalypse Now* (about the Viet Nam War), General Corman (played by G. D. Spradlin) utters these memorable lines: ". . . there's a conflict in every human heart, between the rational and the irrational, between good and evil, and good does not always triumph. Sometimes, the dark side overcomes what Lincoln called the better angels of our nature." Human history is in many ways a story about giving in to the dark side. At every level of our existence, whether within ourselves, between and among ourselves, or environmentally and globally, we experience disharmony and strife. Revelation assumes free moral agents responsible to their Creator for their actions (Rev 3:20; 21:7–8; 22:12–17). But what should not be missed in all this is the truly good news of Revelation: there will be a glorious outcome to this state of conscious and cosmic conflict. The New Jerusalem is a glittering image of harmony, unity, and perfect equilibrium. We'll say more about that later. For now we need to take a long hard look at the battle between good and evil as played out in John's prophecy to the seven churches in Asia Minor.

Revelation is essentially a story about a cosmic power struggle. In spite of God's sovereignty, not all are willing to submit to his reign. In fact, the book features a hostile individual who seeks to supplant God's rule over planet earth. Chapter 12 graphically depicts that person, Satan, as a hideous red dragon and describes his failed planetary coup. As John writes to the churches in Asia Minor, he wants them to understand that the struggle they're facing is nothing new. Satan has been engaged in a battle with God's people, and their struggles are just part of that battle between good and evil that will continue until Jesus returns.

A brief review of the arrangement of the book of Revelation will help us see the past, present, and future elements of the battle between good and evil. After the seven seals are broken (6:1—8:1) and the seven trumpets are blown (8:2—11:15), John pauses the story and zooms out. His intent appears to be to provide a "big picture" perspective on what's going on and why. In other words, John is not necessarily presenting a chronology of future events. Chapter 12 is a master key for unlocking the interpretation of the entire book. Here we are introduced to three key players in the story of redemption:

- A woman

- An enormous red dragon

- A male child

The first key person in the drama is, fittingly, a woman. It was, after all, Eve who was deceived by the serpent in the garden of Eden (Gen 3:1–6; 2 Cor 11:3; 2 Tim 2:14). The Lord promises Eve that her offspring will crush the head of the serpent (Gen 3:15; cf. Rom 16:20). Is then the woman of Rev 12 Eve? Or is the woman the Virgin Mary who gives birth to "a male child who will rule all the nations" (Rev 12:5), almost certainly a reference to Jesus? Though both suggestions are plausible, neither quite fits the precise description of the woman in chapter 12.

1. In the first place, the woman is called "a wondrous sign," a description suggesting more than a solitary individual.

2. Second, she is described as "clothed with the sun, with the moon under her feet and a crown of twelve stars on her head." Her attire reminds us of a story from the book of Genesis. The story tells about a dream Joseph had when he was seventeen years old (Gen 37). He saw the sun and moon and eleven stars bow down before him (Gen 37:9). His father Jacob interprets that to mean that he and Joseph's mother along with the eleven other sons would bow down to Joseph (Gen 37:10). Jacob thus infers that he, whose name had already been changed to Israel (Gen 32:28), is the sun, his wife is the moon, and the eleven stars are Jacob's other sons. Assuming that Rev 12:1 adapts Gen 37:9, we suggest that the woman of Rev 12 represents Israel, the people of God.

3. Third, "she was pregnant and cried out in pain as she was about to give birth" (Rev 12:2). Her circumstances are even more decisively in favor of our identification of this woman as Israel. In several Old Testament passages, the nation of Israel or Judah is depicted as a woman undergoing the pangs of child birth (Isa 26:17; 54:1; 66:7; Mic 4:3), which is

Some scholars have suggested that John adapts a bit of ancient astrology for his purposes. The Jewish background for our text may be found in one of the famous Dead Sea Scrolls. In a text called *Thanksgiving Hymns*, and dating to the first century B.C., there is a passage describing the birth of Messiah: "She who is big with the Man of distress is in her pains. For she shall give birth to a man-child in the billows of Death, and in the bonds of Sheol there shall spring from the crucible of the pregnant one a Marvellous Counsellor with his might; and he shall deliver every man from the billows because of Her who is big with him" (1QH 3.9–10). What this demonstrates is that before the time of Christ a Jewish expectation of a Messiah whose birth would be attended by trying circumstances already existed. This grows out of the Old Testament prophetic promises of a royal prince from the line of David who would deliver Israel from her enemies (Isa 7:14; 9:6–7; Mic 5:2). John's vision reflects a similar expectation, though now understood from a Christian perspective.

precisely where the main emphasis falls in John's vision of this celestial woman—she gives birth to a child who will rule the world.

Most scholars assume that this woman is a representative, collective figure since, after the male child is caught up to heaven, the dragon directs his venom at this woman and "against the rest of her offspring—those who keep God's commands and hold fast their testimony about Jesus" (Rev 12:17). These offspring must surely be Christians who are in a very real sense a continuation of Israel. In short, the woman symbolizes that larger entity, of which Eve was the ancestress and Mary a shining example, namely, the people of God, the true Israel—the people from whom the Messiah comes (Rom 9:5).

Since there can be little doubt that the male child is Jesus, and on this nearly all commentators agree, a good case can be made for the representative nature of this extraordinary woman, the "Queen of Heaven." To this we add that the woman depicted in Rev 17, the prostitute Babylon the Great, is almost certainly a symbolic figure, providing a stark contrast to the symbolic woman of Rev 12 who is also depicted as the resplendent bride of Christ later on in Rev 19:6–9; 21:9–14; 22:17.

Though foreign to highly individualistic, Western thought, ancient Israel assumed the notion of what might be called corporate personality. That is, an individual is viewed as bound up in a community of persons and in a realistic sense lives on in his or her descendants. There are numerous examples of this concept throughout the Bible, especially in the prophets. One finds a classic case in Hos 12:2–6 where the passage should be read on two levels, namely the story of Jacob in Genesis and the story of Jacob's descendants in Hosea's own day during the 8th century B.C. There is a "like ancestor, like descendant" dynamic in this passage. What is true of the individual is true of his descendants.

Something similar to this seems to be what is happening in Revelation 12. Both in terms of corporate solidarity and typologically, Eve lives on in faithful Israel and is exemplified in that remarkable woman upon whom special favor was shown, namely Mary (Luke 1:28, 30, 35). But the primary focus of the figure is collective Israel and its continuance in the church of Jesus Christ. In fact, Paul's theology assumes this corporate dimension. Believers are now "in Christ" and share in his death, burial and resurrection (Rom 6).

Secondly, we are introduced to the primary antagonist, the arch-villain of the overarching story in the Bible. No surprise that John employs the image of a dragon to describe this sinister figure. We recall that in the first book of the Bible a serpent slithers into the garden of Eden (Gen 3). Dragons and serpents typically represent creatures that are both cunning and deadly.

In the ancient Near East, this archetypal fear was personified in a female deity depicted as a hideous dragon. The Canaanites took over this notion and called this being Rahab (not to be confused with the woman who lived in Jericho in Joshua's day), or Leviathan, the monster of the sea. Similar myths occur in ancient Egyptian (Isis, Set or Typhon and Horus) and Greco-Roman (Leto, Python and Apollo) traditions. Echoes of this myth reverberate in the Old Testament (Job 26:12–13; Pss 74:12–17; 89:9–10; Isa 27:1; 51:9; Ezek 29:3; 32:2). Even if the Hebrew writers didn't believe in the real personal existence of such beings, they did borrow the imagery in order to declare the Lord's complete victory over all evil forces that might rise up against his purposes. For example, the Egyptian Pharaoh was sometimes personified as a dragon in the poetry of Israel (Isa 51:9–10). The Lord smashes the heads of the dragon, reflected historically in the account of the plagues upon Egypt and the crossing of the Red Sea. By the way, the Pharaohs of Egypt typically wore a headdress crowned by a coiled Cobra, called the Uraeus. This historicizing of ancient myths helps us understand some of the particular features of Revelation 12.

So who is this enormous red dragon? John doesn't leave us in the dark to speculate: he unmasks the dragon as "that ancient serpent called the devil, or Satan, who leads the whole world astray" (Rev 12:7). And what does he want? The continuation of this draconian drama in chapter 13 contains clues as to his grandiose scheme. He wants to be worshipped as God alone is worshipped (Rev 13:4). He despises God and does all he can to discredit him (Rev 13:6). What he craves is unlimited power resulting in adoration and blind submission to his every whim (Rev 13:16).

The readers in cities such as Smyrna would have connected the dots quickly. Satan craves to be worshipped just as the rulers of Rome craved worship. John was aligning the policies of Rome with the rule of Satan, cluing in his readers that their present struggles were linked to a larger, ancient spiritual battle between God and Satan. Just as the woman was pursued by the dragon, they were being attacked by the present incarnation of the dragon—the Roman Empire.

SATAN: GETTING TO KNOW THE ENEMY

Satan must have possessed a high rank and standing originally. This is inferred from Rev 12:7 where we are told: "And there was war in heaven." War is always a clash of wills. The implication is clear: Satan openly challenged God's power. As a consequence, he lost his place in heaven and was hurled down to earth (Rev 12:8–9). It must be admitted that Scripture is virtually silent about when Satan's rebellion occurred. What is clear is that in Gen 3 he is already opposed to God in that he deceives Eve and succeeds momentarily in winning Adam over to the "dark side" (2 Cor 11:3; 1 Tim 2:14; Rom 5:12–21). The book of Job pictures Satan as having access to the throne of God and ridiculing Job's piety because God favors and protects him (1:6–12).

In Ezek 28:1–19 we have a poetic description of a Canaanite king of Tyre who succumbs to his unbridled ambition for adulation and imagines himself a god during his lifetime on earth (28:2, 6, 9). Contrary to his inflated expectations, he is humbled and brought down to the depths of the underworld (28:8, 10). Even more extraordinary, however are verses 12–19, which many interpreters, ancient and modern, think look beyond the historical Canaanite king and depict the primal fall of this angelic being who was "full of wisdom and perfect in beauty" (28: 12–13). The passage contains several interesting points of similarity to Gen 3 and the Rev 12 drama:

- Lived in Eden, the garden of God (28:13)
- Appointed as a guardian cherub (28:14)
- Lived a blameless life (28:15)
- Fell prey to pride on account of his beauty and splendor (28:12–13, 17)
- Rebelled against God (28:15–16)

- Expelled from God's presence (28:16)

- Will come to a terrible end (28:19)

Whether these passages actually refer to Satan's fall is disputed; perhaps the most we can say is that they at least illustrate the disposition that impelled him to attempt usurping God's sovereignty and majesty. Through this dramatic vision, the stage has been set for the conflict between God's people and Satan—a conflict with deep roots in the past, a particularly sharp sting in the present for the seven churches of Asia Minor, and an undeniable presence in our world today.

Keep in mind that at this point in the book of Revelation, John did not provide a strict chronology of future events. He was pulling back the curtain on spiritual realities that impact what his readers were experiencing. Therefore, John compressed the story of Jesus' life on earth to what was most critical for his readers' situation, showing the power of Jesus over evil. He passes over Jesus' earthly ministry, the arrest and trial, the crucifixion and the resurrection. He moves quickly to his victorious ascension to the throne of God (Rev 12:5; cf. John 17:1–5, 13). At this point, the red dragon, knowing he has been checkmated, attempts a heavenly coup; that too, is quickly quashed. Michael and the good angels give Satan and his allies the boot. He is expelled to earth and that is where he sets up his primary headquarters for resistance to the kingdom of God.

Perhaps this is the moment Jesus was referring to when he told his disciples, "I saw Satan fall like lightning from heaven" (Luke 10:18). The people of God must resist Satan and remain loyal to the true King of Heaven and Earth. This will not be easy: "He [the dragon] is filled with fury, because he knows that his time is short" (Rev 12:13).

We don't want to oversimplify the situation and provide people with an easy excuse: "the devil made me do it!" We are, after all, responsible for our choices. But we do want to emphasize that fallen human nature is mightily assisted in its rebellion by the dragon who hovers in the background. He muddles minds (Rom 1:21–23; 2 Cor 4:4; Eph 4:18) and weakens wills of people who seek to chart their own course without relying on God's word (Jas 4:1–7). In the words of the apostle Peter, "Be alert and of sober mind. Your enemy the devil prowls around like a roaring lion looking for someone to devour. Resist him standing firm in the faith, because you know that your fellow believers throughout the world are undergoing the same kind of sufferings" (1 Pet 5:8–9).

The dragon makes assertions and promises he can't possibly keep: "You will not certainly die . . . your eyes will be opened and you will be like God" (Gen 3:5); "I will give you all their authority and splendor; it has been given to me, and I can give it to anyone I want to. If you worship me, it will all be yours" (Luke 4:6). Whether by hostile persecution or deceptive promises, the goal of Satan is the destruction of God's people.

While Satan works to discourage and destroy, the Scriptures point us toward God's plan for overcoming evil: "Love the Lord your God with all your heart and with all your soul and with all your strength" (Deut 6:5) and "love your neighbor as yourself" (Lev 19:18). Jesus gave his followers this timeless advice: "seek first his kingdom and his righteousness, and all these things will be given to you as well" (Matt 6:33). This call to faithfulness in the midst of pressure is what John advises in Revelation: "This calls for patient endurance on the part of the people of God who keep his commands and remain faithful to Jesus" (14:12). No matter how hard Satan, the Romans, or hostile neighbors press, hang on to the love of God and the hope of his coming kingdom.

One of the purposes of the book Revelation is to expose the dragon's dirty deeds. The telltale signs of his malign activity already appear in the messages to the seven churches of Asia (Rev 2–3). For the most part, the members of the seven house churches are struggling with their own lower natures, but the red dragon lurks behind the scenes.

SATAN'S STRATEGIES

Of the seven churches in Asia Minor, the church at Smyrna had clearly come under satanic attack. The risen Christ, fully aware of their affliction (Rev 2:9), forewarns them: "Do not fear what you are about to suffer. Beware, the devil is about to throw some of you into prison so that you may be tested, and for ten days you will have persecution" (Rev 2:10). Because the believers in Smyrna refused to participate in the imperial cult, they were denounced as unpatriotic and imprisoned for treason.

Likewise, believers in Pergamum had to deal with the imperial cult and a great altar to Zeus on the acropolis overlooking the city. No wonder the Lord refers to Pergamum as the place where "Satan's throne is" (Rev 2:13). One Christian named Antipas had already paid with his life for not participating in the idolatrous rites of the imperial and pagan cults (Rev 2:13). The first readers of the book of Revelation doubtless latched on to

Christ's words concerning the woman: "[she] was given the two wings of an eagle so that she could fly from the serpent into the wilderness, to her place where she is nourished for a time, and times, and half a time" (12:14). Though the dragon makes war against them, they cling to the promise of the Savior: "the gates of Hades will not prevail against [my church]" (Matt 16:18).

Of course, Satan has many faces and multiple strategies. At Pergamum his devious activity manifested itself in individuals promoting the teachings of Balaam and the Nicolaitans (Rev 2:14–15). While certainty about their identity and teaching is lacking, they apparently advocated compromise on certain issues like eating food offered to idols and sexual morality. The church at Thyatira had a notorious prophetess whom John gave the nickname "Jezebel," recalling the wicked, Canaanite queen of King Ahab (1 Kgs 16:29–33; 18:4; 19:1–2; 21:1–26; 2 Kgs 9:30–37). She blatantly disregarded church standards on sexual morality and even advertised her teaching as "Satan's deep secrets" (Rev 2:20, 24). False teachers are accountable for their own actions and teachings, but their presence in the midst of the house churches reminds us of the apostle Peter's warning to believers also located in Asia: "the devil prowls around like a roaring lion looking for someone to devour" (2 Pet 5:8).

Revelation 13 further explores Satan's attempts to annihilate the church of Jesus Christ. Now believers must stare into the evil eyes of the enraged dragon. The struggle between good and evil arrives at a climactic moment. The chapter begins with an ominous scene. The red dragon conjures up from the depths of the sea a terrifying beast. Here John adapts imagery earlier used by the prophet Daniel. Daniel's vision predicted the rise of four successive world powers portrayed as ferocious animals, the fourth of which was exceedingly terrifying (Dan 7:1–7). John combines elements of these animals into one frightening beast energized by the dragon himself (Rev 13:1–2).

Interpreters are generally agreed that the beast is the antichrist referred to by John in his first epistle (1 John 2:18; cf. 2 John 7) and the man of lawlessness described by Paul (2 Thess 2:3–4). It is possible that the first readers of Revelation saw this beast rising from the sea as a symbol of the Roman Empire, but today we can also see how the characteristics of the beast could be applied to many world powers we have seen and expect to see in the future. However we classify the beast, he plays an important role in the dragon's counterattack:

- The dragon creates an unholy trinity: Satan, antichrist, and the false prophet, a crude imitation of the Holy Trinity of Father, Son, and Holy Spirit.

- The dragon counterfeits the resurrection of Christ: "One of the heads of the beast seemed to have had a fatal wound, but the fatal wound had been healed. The whole world was filled with wonder and followed the beast" (Rev 13:3–4).

- The dragon blasphemes God, conquers believers and controls the entire planet (Rev 13:5–7).

- The dragon imposes worldwide worship of the beast who is in his own image (Rev 13:8)

- The dragon conjures another beast who mockingly imitates the Lamb (Christ) and serves as a sort of propaganda minister on behalf of the beast and his evil empire (Rev 13:11–15).

- The dragon imposes strict economic control over the world in order to coerce complete compliance and cooperation (Rev 13:16–18).

To those looking at the surface, evil has apparently triumphed. Satan's aspiration to be worshipped as God is achieved. The rebellion is complete. But is it? There are pockets of resistance on the unseen margins and a completely different story once you go below the surface. John writes that "all inhabitants of the earth will worship the beast—all whose names have not been written in the Lamb's book of life" (Rev 13:8). But we are already told that a vast multitude have their names written in the Lamb's book of life and have God's name and the name of the Lamb sealed on their foreheads (Rev 7; 14:1). These individuals refuse to accept the mark of the beast and, as a consequence, the dragon launches an all-out assault on them. If allowed to continue, he would surely succeed in ridding the earth of all believers. At this darkest moment in the history of the church, the tide suddenly changes. To borrow an image from C. S. Lewis' story about Narnia, Aslan is on the move![1] But we save the last battle for the last chapter!

---

1. The reader will probably recognize this as a reference to C. S. Lewis's masterpiece *The Lion, the Witch and the Wardrobe.*

HOW DO WE "FIGHT" EVIL TODAY?

If there is a "resistance movement" among the followers of the Lamb, how do they, in this hour of deepest crisis, confront the monstrous evil of the dragon? The answer may surprise you.

We've already touched on the answer offered in Revelation. Now we want to make it clear and explicit. The first thing we must come to grips with is that the book of Revelation is *not* a rousing call to resist force with force, to take up arms, and seek a military victory over the evil empire or the subjects of the evil empire. The message is quite clear: "Whoever has ears to hear, let them hear. If anyone is to go into captivity, into captivity they will go. If anyone is to be killed with the sword, with the sword they will be killed. This calls for patient endurance and faithfulness on the part of God's people" (Rev 13:9–10). John's message for the seven churches is that suffering is coming, but new life with Christ awaits all who endure the current tribulation at the hands of the Romans. John wants his readers to wait patiently.

Reading this today, our protests can hardly be stifled. This is crazy! Surely, we are entitled to self-defense! And it certainly does not accord with "the American way"! We may argue that Christians must take up arms and attack the antichrist. But this is not what the book of Revelation says.

God's path to victory has already been dramatically portrayed in the throne room scene (Rev 5). There the victorious Lamb appeared with the sign of his throat having been slit, just like the Passover lamb and the many lambs sacrificed to the Lord in ancient Israel (Rev 5:6). The salutation of the book opens with a doxology addressed to Jesus Christ, "him who loves us and freed us from our sins by his blood" (Rev 1:5). Yes, we reply, we understand that. Christ saved us by his self-giving sacrifice, an incredible demonstration of love (Rom 5:6–11), but what should we do about the evil in our world?

We do not resist evil by adopting the same tools, weapons, and strategies as the forces of evil in our world. If the legions of Rome attacked believers, Christians were not permitted to form their own army in order to "defeat" the evil they embodied. Revelation shows that the dragon seemingly controls the planet, and we can certainly relate to this depiction of affairs even today. Whether by deception or outright violence, Satan is working hard to destroy God's people. John's gory description of the great whore Babylon depicts the extent of the carnage: "the woman was drunk with the blood of the saints and the blood of the witnesses to Jesus" (Rev

17:6). All human attempts to resist Satan's evil by violence are useless then, now, and in the future.

How then in circumstances like these ought the people of God to respond? John sets us straight: "These are they who have come out of the great ordeal; they have washed their robes and made them white in the blood of the Lamb" (Rev 7:14). In other words, they continue to testify and die for their faith and trust God to overturn evil once and for all since the Lamb has already won the decisive victory. In Rev 12, after Satan is cast down to earth, an angelic voice proclaims the key to victory over evil: ". . . they have conquered him [the dragon] by the blood of the Lamb and by the word of their testimony, *for they did not cling to life even in the face of death*" (Rev 12:11; italics for emphasis).[2] This reminds us of Jesus' teaching: "For those who want to save their life will lose it, and those who lose their life for my sake will find it" (Matt 16:25). The apostle Peter finally grasped this great truth: "For to this you have been called because Christ also suffered for you, leaving you an example, so that you should follow in his steps" (1 Pet 2:21).[3]

Is that then the last word on the battle between good and evil? What about the perpetrators of evil and those who give in to the dark side and bear the mark of the beast? They will assuredly stand trial before the one who sits on the great white throne and receive their just punishment (Rev 20:11–13; cf. Rev 14:9–11; 16:4–7; 18:4–8). The fifth seal portrays the martyrs under the altar praying: "Sovereign Lord, holy and true, how long will it be before you judge and avenge our blood on the inhabitants of the earth?" (Rev 6:10). We may imagine the Christians in the seven churches of Asia Minor calling out to God, "How long must Rome persecute us and put us to death?"

The answer is: "a little longer, until the number would be complete . . ." (Rev 6:11). Anchored in hope, the saints patiently endure the assaults of the dragon in all its manifestations: "Here is a call for the endurance of the saints, those who keep the commandments of God and hold fast to the faith of Jesus" (Rev 14:12). Those who remain faithful are comforted and

---

2. "The proclamation of the Gospel will always be marked by the sign of the Cross—this is what each generation of Jesus' disciples must learn anew. The Cross is and remains the sign of 'the Son of Man': ultimately, in the battle against lies and violence, truth and love have no other weapon than the witness of suffering" (Pope Benedict XVI, *Jesus of Nazareth: Part Two: Holy Week* [San Francisco: Ignatius, 2011] 49).

3. "In most of our human definitions, victory includes survival. But the Bible knows better. It often grants victory to those who seem thoroughly crushed, viciously destroyed" (David Allan Hubbard, *The Second Coming* [Downers Grove, IL: InterVarsity, 1984] 68).

reassured: "they will rest from their labors, for their deeds follow them" (Rev 14:13).

In conclusion, the people of God must keep three things clearly in mind:

- Vengeance belongs to the Lord (Rev 6:9–11; 19:2). The apostle Paul agrees with John: "Beloved, never avenge yourselves, but leave room for the wrath of God; for it is written, 'Vengeance is mine, I will repay, says the Lord'" (Rom 12:19, quoting Deut 32:35) and so does the apostle Peter: "Do not repay evil with evil or insult with insult. On the contrary, repay evil with blessings, because to this you were called so that you may inherit a blessing" (1 Pet 3:9; cf. 2:13–23; 4:1, 12–19). This is the way our Master taught us to live (Matt 5:38–42).

- Evil will not triumph in the end. God's wrath is a reality and should never to be taken lightly (Rom 1:18). Before the last bowl judgments are poured out on the evil empire, an angel announces impending punishment upon those who accept the mark of the beast: "fire and sulfur in the presence of the holy angels and in the presence of the Lamb . . . and the smoke of their torment goes up forever and ever" (Rev 14:10–11).

- Believers overcome evil by what seems counterintuitive, heeding the exhortation of the risen Christ: "Be faithful until death, and I will give you the crown of life" (Rev 2:10).

While many of those living under the boot of Rome and its brutal military pledged their allegiance to Caesar and worshipped him in order to survive, John has a shocking message for the churches under his care. They cannot give in to Rome—Satan is behind the power of Rome and the persecution they're enduring. They cannot fight back—Jesus already fought the evil spiritual forces behind Rome and has triumphed. Escape is not an option; neither is forming a separate resistance movement. They must hold on because all is not as it seems.

Contrary to everything they could see around them, the Christians of Asia Minor had already triumphed over Satan and Rome through Christ. God's reward is waiting for them, which is the ultimate mark of his victory over the forces of evil. Better yet, God's victory described in Revelation isn't just true for the original readers. While the original readers certainly saw their struggle against Rome in the images of Revelation, John is also providing us with a glimpse into the climax of history where the forces of evil make their end run to overthrow God's rule.

John's message is the same for each succeeding generation of believers, especially the last one, "those who are left till the coming of the Lord" (1 Thess 4:15). God will triumph over evil, whether that's a human government or the unseen spiritual powers in our world. There is a battle against evil that must still be fought. We experience glimpses of it when we fight our own battles against temptation or the deception of Satan, but we have not yet witnessed the complete triumph of God. John assures us that even though we are surrounded by unmistakable evidence that Satan and his evil minions are at work in our world, God has already determined the outcome of this battle. Although difficult days remain in the future and the power of Satan will at times be displayed, there is a greater power at work in our world that has already overcome. Waiting will not be easy with the forces of evil on the prowl, but we must remain patient, trusting that God is able to fulfill his promises.

SECTION 5

Hope for the Future

Chapter 9

A New Journey Begins

LYDIA LEANED OVER THE scroll, reading the final lines over and over again. She had so many questions for Philip. It had been another long sleepless night, and the scroll had provided a welcome diversion.

The first night after her husband's execution, she gave his clothing to her servant, asking him to donate them to the beggars by the town gate. She'd held onto his sandals. She wasn't sure why. Maybe she just needed a small reminder of his presence.

The night after that, she'd wandered between her own room and the room where her three sons struggled to fall asleep. Every night passed with Lydia either staring at the ceiling as she fought to calm her mind or bustling around the house by dim candlelight. Now, with this scroll to read, Lydia welcomed the distraction from her daily worries about money, food, and the unthinkable terror that the Romans could come for her boys next.

Since the soldiers had dragged her husband away, her home felt like an unfamiliar land where she didn't quite know how to exist. Her home had never looked better. The floor was swept and washed. All of the torn fabric had been mended. Everything by the hearth hung in its place, clean and ready for use. For all that Lydia had perfected on the outside, her heart ached and her mind swirled with thoughts of survival. As much as she feared leaving her home, she also found it unsettling. On more than one occasion she'd considered either taking in someone from the church to live in the spare room where her guest now slept. Then again, relocating to a smaller home where she could avoid the glare of the officials who had framed her husband held a greater appeal.

As the rising sun made it easier to read the scroll in front of her, she traced her finger over the small letters once again. One particular line caught her eye every time, "He will wipe away every tear." She thought of the lonely nights crying by herself and those moments before bedtime where her boys cried out for their father. They didn't feel safe. She didn't feel safe. She didn't know how much more she could take. While the details were vague about God's new home for his people, she couldn't stop reading about Jesus wiping away every tear. As good as that sounded for some day, she needed that now. She needed God to step in and deliver her. She needed God to protect and provide for her boys.

Lydia startled at the sound of a moving chair.

"Oh, hello, Philip."

"I see you found the scroll."

"Yes, I'm so grateful you left it out. It has been a welcome diversion. You know about my husband?"

Philip nodded.

"It's all been more than I can bear."

"You've had it especially bad here. I'm sorry for your loss."

"Thank you," Lydia said, wiping her eyes. "I'm sure you've seen your fair share of losses as you've traveled."

"Yes. The Romans have been quite aggressive in some towns. John's letter has comforted many."

"What can you tell me about this letter?" asked Lydia. "I've been over it a few times through the night."

"I suppose it means quite a few different things," replied Philip. "In some ways, it's about God's plans for us now, but in another sense, it's giving us some hints about the future and the hope of being reunited with Christ one day."

"It's all one big mess to me."

Philip laughed. "You're not the first to say that."

"What do you think it means?" Lydia replied.

"I'll do my best. Is there anything in particular that you wanted to talk about?"

Lydia unrolled the scroll and pointed at a section near the end. "I want to know what this New Jerusalem is. What does it mean that God will be the temple? And why is there a tree being used for the healing of nations?"

"I was afraid you were going to ask about the lake of fire."

"Honestly," replied Lydia, "I can think of a few soldiers and politicians I'd like to send there right now."

"Right. Well, the point of this letter is that God is already victorious. We just don't see it yet. However, there will come a day when God visibly rules. We don't know what this New Jerusalem will look like, but the point is that Rome's days are numbered. While we need to persevere for today, there will come a day when God will reward us with his presence and peace, wiping away every tear."

"So where is my husband right now?"

"He's with the Lord right now, but he will be in that city with us one day. Jesus is preparing a home for us as he promised, and that new home will be this New Jerusalem you read about. We live in fear of the Romans for now, but God will overthrow them one day."

Lydia nodded. "And the tree of life?"

"We read about it in the book of Genesis. It symbolizes God's restoration of humanity and the eternal life God grants us. We won't ever know the sting of death again."

"Death is so terrible."

"I can't imagine how hard your life is right now," replied Philip.

"I need to keep going for my boys." Lydia looked over the scroll again. Philip watched as her finger slipped along each line.

"You've given me quite a bit to think about. Thank you, Philip."

He smiled and nodded.

"You know, you're a pretty good preacher," Lydia said. "You ever think about doing that?"

"Oh, I'm only good for small groups," Philip replied.

"That's all we've got left here. You'd do fine."

"Except for the part where all of your pastors have been killed by the Romans," Philip replied. "I'm not a brave man."

"Nonsense!" Lydia snapped. "You've brought this letter to all seven churches. You've hidden it from the Romans. You've walked through all kinds of weather and risked being robbed. You're plenty brave by just about anyone's standards."

Philip's face reddened.

"I'm just saying that the church has lost a lot of great teachers, and someone like you could make a real difference. In fact, you already know people in all of the seven churches. Maybe you need to do something else now that the letter has been delivered. Maybe you need to make sure the churches stick to John's teaching. If they're going to make it, they need reminders that God is going to deliver them some day from the boot of Rome. I know I need that reminder."

"But who am I to be the one to follow up on this letter?" Philip replied. Lydia could see her suggestion had made Philip uncomfortable. Doing so may have made her a bad host, but her husband had told her she had the gift of prophecy. Perhaps this feeling in her gut about Philip was more than a feeling. Perhaps she needed to give him the confidence he needed to take this leap of faith.

"I'll tell you who you are," Lydia said. "You yourself told me that John sent this letter to you. You were the trusted carrier he chose to bring this message in the first place. Do you question John's judgment?"

"Honestly, yes, sometimes I do." Philip hung his head. "It's a burden. It's not easy to know that such an important letter depends completely on me. I was hoping I could get away from it for a while."

"Well, the good news is that it doesn't completely depend on you anymore. You've given it to all of the churches. It's safely copied and is being taught as we speak. But we both know that tough days remain ahead. We need you to help us remain faithful."

Philip looked at Lydia hard, his eyes taking on a fierce quality that made her afraid for a moment. Had she offended him?

"I know you're right. Someone at the last church suggested it. I've just been fighting it. I've never thought of myself as a preacher. And I really am terrified of the Romans. I don't see myself surviving very long as a pastor these days."

"Unless God wants to use you to help his church survive this season. Either way, isn't the point of this letter that God is with us no matter how difficult things become?"

Philip nodded.

As Lydia stood up to serve Philip breakfast, she noticed his sandals were worn out, pieced together with random strips of leather. She picked up her husband's sandals from the corner where she'd stashed them and offered them to Philip.

"I couldn't part with these after they took my husband," she said, "but now I know that God was saving them for you."

Chapter 10

A Better Ending to the Story

IN THIS CHAPTER

- Reasons for caution when interpreting Revelation's conclusion.
- How Revelation uses themes in the rest of the Bible.
- The future God is planning for his people in the New Jerusalem.

WITH POPULAR BOOKS AND movies today that focus on the rapture, apocalyptic battles, global destruction, and even the militarizing of a Christian remnant, it is understandable that Revelation has left many readers puzzled about how this unusual book fits alongside the narratives, prophecies, and letters that precede it. It is rarely on the reading list for any Bible study or Sunday school class. Readers of the New Testament, especially those who are new to the Bible, find it particularly jarring to move from a series of straightforward letters into a series of visions that strike them as both violent and terrifying. Those familiar with the Bible's major themes can understandably wonder about some of today's more popular teachings on Revelation: Didn't Jesus come to initiate the arrival of God's kingdom on earth rather than rapturing his followers away? Why would God destroy the creation that he called "good"? If Jesus defeated evil on the cross, why does Satan seem so powerful in Revelation?

These are just a few of the reasons why Revelation is so easy to skip. It baffles us and doesn't seem to fit with everything else we've just read in the Bible—let alone provide the kind of ending we would expect for the Bible. Tying all of the Bible's great themes into a fitting conclusion is no small matter, and perhaps John never intended to write the "last book of the Bible." However, there is no reason why Revelation should diverge from what we have just read in the previous sixty-five books.

If Revelation is inspired scripture, we should expect to find a family resemblance to the narratives, poems, and prophecies that precede it. That, in fact, is what we find. John was offering hope for both the present and the future to the seven churches in Asia Minor. John provided a glimpse of what is to come while also opening the eyes of his readers to the spiritual realities around them. John most likely mingled his present situation and the future in his images and symbols. In addition, each revelation of spiritual realities or prediction of the future certainly has a connection with what has come before it in the biblical story. In fact, the end of Revelation is particularly rich with references to the garden of Eden, the exodus, prophetic writings, and the words of Jesus.

For all of the connections we can make to the great narrative in Scripture, the future hope presented in Revelation remains shrouded in mystery. In fact, the debates today over what is to come have unfortunately overshadowed what Revelation could have meant to its original readers and what it could teach us. By focusing on future forecasts, we can miss the practical truths about the victory of Christ, the real presence of evil in our world, and the hope of God's final victory. John's original readers certainly used Revelation to look ahead, but they also found comforting words about the present victory of God over evil. John's predictions had a present/future meaning, much like the present/future tension of the kingdom.

Jesus is King today, but his rule will not be fully manifested until the future. John certainly predicted a future return of God. There is no doubt that tumultuous events and suffering will precede that return—just ask the seven churches in Asia Minor about that! However, debates remain about just how literal events such as the plagues, bowls of wrath, Millennium, or final battle against Satan will be.

Some, like Ed, believe many of the dramatic plagues, natural disasters, and wars in Revelation are primarily symbolic, speaking to the tumultuous nature or our world without necessarily corresponding to specific events. They stand for cycles of what has been, what is today, and what is to come until Jesus returns. Others, like Larry, primarily link the events of Revelation with the future—a time when evil makes its last gasp attempt to throw off the rule of God and God unleashes his judgment against sin and evil. Our two perspectives here differ primarily by a matter of degree. The powers of evil are no doubt warring against God's people as they have been throughout history, and there's no reason to suspect they'll give up until the return of Jesus. Will the powers of evil concentrate their efforts in one dramatic ending or will Jesus simply return? However the future unfolds, the key points before us remain:

1. No one knows when Jesus will return. Attempting to forecast the end of the world or to determine whether we are living in the last days is doomed to frustration and failure.

2. The focus of Revelation was to encourage suffering believers to persevere because Jesus was still ruling over a chaotic world and Jesus will return to overthrow evil, judge their oppressors, and visibly rule on earth.

3. Revelation celebrates the victory of God and prompts God's people to worship in the midst of suffering and uncertainty.

There is much to explore from point two as we look at the way Revelation resolves the key themes of the Bible. Rather than ending the Bible on a wild, chaotic note, it provides a resolution that we've all been longing for—even if the process of resolving God's judgment of evil leaves us a bit perplexed. However, before we can grasp the hope presented in Revelation, we need to let go of some interpretations that have only added to the confusion about this book.

REASONS FOR CAUTION ABOUT THE END OF REVELATION

Predicting the future based on biblical texts is particularly tricky, and the people of God have always struggled to pinpoint specific outcomes in the future based on prophecies or other predictions. Before we make any statements about the Millennium, Final Judgment, or New Jerusalem, we should review the track record of past generations when it comes to making forecasts based on Scripture.

That track record, if anything, leaves us cautious about placing too much stock in any one prediction. The reception of Jesus by his contemporaries stands as exhibit A. The Jews who read the prophets imagined that a "victorious" Messiah would deliver them from their enemies and set up

God's kingdom. They expected the Messiah to meticulously keep the law, banish Gentile sinners from the land, and usher in a golden age. If we read the same prophetic texts, it's easy to understand why many struggled to recognize Jesus as the Messiah. The coming Messiah and the return of God's rule to the land read as one in the same.

When Jesus arrived on the scene, no one had any idea that the Messiah would be God incarnate, suffer on a cross, and rise from the dead. No one thought the Messiah would abolish parts of the Law (by fulfilling it) and welcome in sinners and Gentiles. Many of the things that Jesus did in fulfillment of the Scriptures struck his contemporaries as completely wrong.

Before we make too much of our interpretations of Revelation, particularly as related to the return of Jesus, history suggests that we have plenty of reasons to remain open to the mystery surrounding the "events" in Revelation. Historically, the church has struggled to arrive at any kind of consensus about what the return of Jesus will involve. Starting with an expectation that Jesus would manifest himself at any moment among the early church, interpretations shifted between the more literal to the symbolic in the centuries that followed.

Belief in the rapture captured the imagination of many Christians in the 1830s through the teachings of John Nelson Darby. As belief in the rapture took hold among American Christians, we find story after story of Christians who sold all of their earthly possessions, donned white robes, and waited on hillsides when pastors predicted a specific date for the rapture. The most well-known rapture prediction is the Great Disappointment in 1844, which was prompted by William Miller's prediction for the return of Christ.

Today we have novels that predict how the final ending will unfold as well as video series that explain how the events in Revelation are linked with the modern state of Israel and the temple mount. Tourists visit the Valley of Megiddo in order to "preview" the site of the final battle between God and the forces of evil. Lost in this speculation over details is the message John communicated to the seven churches and to us about God's final dealings with evil and the fulfillment of Scripture's promises through the Millennium and the New Jerusalem. It is a classic case of missing the forest for the trees. Let's take a step back from the details at the end of Revelation in order to clear up some common misconceptions so that we can focus on what John was trying to communicate.

WHAT REVELATION IS NOT

It can be quite jarring to read the message in 1 John that focuses on loving one another and then flip a few pages only to find wars, beasts, a white throne of judgment, a dragon, and a "new heavens and new earth" dropping from the sky at the end of Revelation. As we look at Revelation as inspired scripture that fits into the larger narrative of Scripture, which tells us how God is redeeming humanity, we should expect to find a certain amount of continuity with the ways and goals of God. Any interpretation of Revelation that suggests God has made an about-face should send up a red flag and lead us to search for explanations that are more in keeping with what we know from the first sixty-five books.

Revelation Is Not an Escape from Earth.

This is probably one of the most tragic results that have come from mis-readings of Revelation that have linked the rapture with the time of Christ's return. Coupling the rapture with a focus on "going to heaven when you die" has led to an overemphasis on God removing Christians from a dangerous world that God will destroy at the end of time. This focus on escape from this world has fed into a church vs. culture mentality in many Christian quarters.

By focusing on escape, the central idea of Revelation and of the Scriptures is clouded: God is coming to dwell among his creation to bring restoration and peace. In fact, once we step back from the focus on being saved just to go to heaven, we can see that Revelation shows us how God restores people to the kinds of lives on earth that God had intended all along. The sanctification of the Holy Spirit among us today is, in fact, preparing us for that kind of restored life with God and with one another. What we experience as a foretaste with God today will one day be our reality on a restored earth. John wrote Revelation because he knew the seven churches in Asia needed encouragement to endure the hardships coming their way and "escape" was not an option. If anything, John wanted his readers to imitate the incarnation of Christ and to endure evil, trusting in the victory of the Lamb of God. The victory did not require an evacuation from a dangerous world. In fact, the battle against evil had already been won, and God's invasion has been well underway ever since.

SECTION 5: Hope for the Future

Christians Are Not Waging War

Some popular interpretations of Revelation speculate that believers will one day organize an active, physical resistance against Satan and his "allies" on earth. This view is troubling because it both misses critically important themes throughout the New Testament and Revelation in particular. Although Revelation describes the kings of the earth as organizing for battle and the dragon attempts to kill the woman and child, Revelation shows us that the Lamb of God is sitting on the throne, uncontested in his victory.

While the seven churches saw chaos all around them and suffered at the point of the spear of the Roman army, they were not in a position to take up arms against them. They were not fighting for a stake in the Roman political system. They also were not fighting against their neighbors. To accept an "us vs. them" mentality completely undermines the focus on the Gospels and the book of Acts where the church is sent out into the world. Far from viewing the world as a place for cultural or political battles, the world is a place where God's people must persevere as faithful witnesses until the return of their victorious Lord.

The opening letters to the seven churches focus on encouraging them to hold on in the midst of trying circumstances, not in fighting back. While the hope of Jesus' return is certainly present throughout Revelation, the image of the Lamb who has overcome is a source of hope for a suffering, persevering church. The war between God and the serpent has already been fought and won when Jesus died on the cross and rose from the dead. Revelation describes the final stages of this war that has already been won and only awaits a concluding battle. God is not on the verge of losing the fight against evil. The enemy is not at the gates of God's kingdom, even if there are days where Christians feel like evil holds all of the advantages in our world. The last thing John wanted to perpetuate was a fortress mentality or a sense of fear about the power of evil in our world. Revelation keeps showing us the hidden realm of heaven where Christ is the victorious Lord over all until he visibly establishes his rule. The final battle isn't even close to an even fight, and that assurance gives us hope for even our darkest days.

God Is Not Against the World

There is quite a bit of conflict throughout the book of Revelation from wars to plagues. However, these parts of John's vision don't necessarily mean that

God is unleashing a wave of indeterminate destruction on the world that consumes everyone in its path. For example, the presence of angels pouring bowls of wrath and unleashing plagues in the world is intended to call to mind the exodus from Egypt where God afflicted the Egyptians in order to set his people free.

We may fear the "end times" because we read about these plagues and disasters that precede a final battle and judgment. However, the point of Revelation is that God is delivering his people from the powers of evil and any ruling powers on earth aligned with them. God rewards his own people for persevering. However the plagues and bowls of wrath are manifested in our world, Revelation is not suggesting that God has or will ever attack his own people. While we can find stories where God handed over the disobedient Israelites to their oppressors, the focus of Revelation is that God delivers his faithful church as it endures suffering.

As the seven churches prayed for deliverance from Rome, John revealed God's larger plan to judge evil by overthrowing powerful empires like Rome. In fact, the readers of Revelation would have viewed the beast with the seven horns as an image standing for Rome, a city known for its seven hills. The focus of God's wrath is on the beast, the dragon, and their allies. While each person will have to give an account of what he or she has done at the final judgment of the world, it's most likely that the symbols of God's wrath throughout Revelation function much like the plagues in the book of Exodus. God is no doubt caring for his people, and however these dramatic events play out, the goals are to both unseat powerful authorities aligned with Satan and to prompt the world to repent.

Revelation Does Not Describe the Destruction of Creation

There is no mistaking that Revelation presents a dramatic change to the world as we know it, but it's hard to know just how big a change John had in mind. Was he presenting symbols that point to a restoration of the known world or does he have a more complete recreation in mind?

We can be certain that John is not presenting us with the complete "destruction" of the world. Rather, it is a dramatic recreation. Revelation does present some dramatic events happening in the world, but, John's point isn't to describe the destruction of the earth and then point to God replacing it. Keep in mind that creation was described as good, and that creation longs for the return of God. This is not a suicidal desire on the part of creation, and God isn't about to change his mind about what he has made. The key issue here is that God must rid the world of sin.

While the recreation of this world may be dramatic and may involve cataclysmic events, Revelation simply states, "the first heaven and the first earth had passed away" (Rev 21:1). The fire and melting we read about in 2 Peter 3:10 is most likely a reference to God's refining fire that will produce a markedly different world, but the "recreation" process itself will not be destructive even if the end product is significantly different from what we know. God returns to this world after sin and evil have run their course, and he must now do away with sin, chaos, and every power set against him.

For example, when John says that there is no sea, we need to keep in mind that his readers would have viewed the ocean as a place of chaos and uncertainty. It served as a powerful reminder that all people were at the mercy of far more powerful forces—a point that makes Jesus' calming the oceans quite significant for his disciples.[1] In addition, the sea divided God's people from one another. The removal of the "sea" from the restored or "recreated" world is a way of emphasizing the completeness of God's rule and the unity of all people in this new creation.

It's clear that the conclusion to the story of God and his people can be easy to misconstrue thanks to the symbols and imagery used in Revelation. However, when we step back from some of the more sensational interpretations today, we can see that John's resolution to Revelation fulfills many of the hopes woven throughout Scripture. From God's promise to crush the serpent's head, to the hope of God dwelling among his people, to a final judgment where God's people are finally vindicated, Revelation concludes with dramatic images that fulfill the hopes laid out throughout the Old and New Testaments. Now that we have cleared the air a bit, let's take a closer look at what John presents at the conclusion of Revelation.

HOPE FOR THE SEVEN CHURCHES AND FOR US

The millennial reign of Christ and his church emphatically asserts that good finally triumphs over evil on the chessboard of human history. The planetary coup attempted by Satan fails in the end. He is checkmated and swept from the board. The agonized prayer of generations of believers, "How long, O Lord?" receives an answer by the return of the rightful king.

1. I am grateful to Zack Hunt for this particular suggestion about Jesus walking on the water.

Secondly, the world needs to see righteousness actually lived out on earth. The second petition of the Lord's Prayer (really the Disciples' Prayer) requests: "Your kingdom come, Your will be done, on *earth* as it is in heaven" (Matt 6:10; italics for emphasis). At last, God's will is done on earth during Christ's millennial reign. Everyone agrees: human history has been in short supply of righteousness. World history is a dreary recital and repetition of unrelenting unrighteous. Economic and political injustice is the norm rather than the exception of human governance and self-centered and self-seeking attitudes sabotage all human endeavors. What is desperately needed is a demonstration of what true righteousness looks like.

In his famous Sermon on the Mount (Matt 5–7), Jesus sketched out a breathtaking agenda for a righteousness far exceeding mere human standards (Matt 5:20). The Millennium provides a near-perfect setting for such an enterprise. Christ, whose character and behavior defines righteousness, reigns with his glorified saints who reflect this true righteousness in a world exempt from the unrighteous schemes of Satan. It will truly be a place where "righteousness is at home" (2 Pet 3: 13).

Perhaps the most fundamental function of the Millennium comes down to this perennial question: Is God's judgment really fair? In the end, will people get what they deserve? The visible reign of Christ on earth lays this question to rest once and for all. God demonstrates what a holy and righteous kingdom is like—the perfect foil for Rome and every flawed empire that has ever followed. In short, God paroles Satan and permits him access to planet earth (Rev 20:7–10). Predictably, he reverts to form and, incredibly, once again "deceives the nations at the four corners of the earth, Gog and Magog, in order to gather them for battle; they are as numerous as the sands of the sea" (Rev 20:8).

An all-out attack on the holy city is short-lived and quickly quelled. Once again, the saints take no active part in resisting the assault. God's enemies are simply consumed. As for the devil, the jig is up. He has deceived for the last time and now meets his predetermined destiny, which is the "lake of fire and sulfur" (Rev 20:10).

This rebellion after the millennial reign makes a profound point. Ten centuries of righteous rule by the righteous one confirm the words of Jeremiah the prophet: "The heart is devious above all else; it is perverse—who can understand it?" (Jer 17:9). Even after enjoying a time of unprecedented righteousness, peace and prosperity, there are still rebels who want to do it

So who in the world are Gog and Magog? Commentators offer a wide array of possibilities. Popular books like *The Late Great Planet Earth* by Hal Lindsey and the *Left Behind* series by Tim LaHaye and Jerry Jenkins make a connection with Russia. In our opinion, this is quite unlikely. In fact, Google can't help you find Gog! Gog and Magog occur in the book of Ezekiel 38–39 and refer to a legendary king and his territories located in what is today southern Russia. The point is that in the sixth century B.C. this region represented people to the far north, on the very fringes of the known world from the vantage point of ancient Israel. Consequently, we should probably be content in saying that in John's vision they represent the far-flung peoples of the world. Like Adam and Eve in the garden, they fall for the falsehood that they can do better for themselves than by trusting and obeying God. It is a fatal mistake.

"my way." This refusal to render obedience to the true king is a snapshot of human history from the garden of Eden to the fiery finale before the walls of the New Jerusalem. And it illustrates, as perhaps nothing else can, the fairness of God's judgment. Even under near perfect conditions for human existence, the "Magog" multitudes rebel. They have no legitimate excuse. Such folly merits God's judgment. "It is what they deserve! . . . Yes, O Lord God, the Almighty, your judgments are true and just!" (Rev 16:6–7).

After Jesus settles the final victory over evil, John sees the holy city, the New Jerusalem, descending to the new earth. What follows constitutes a climactic moment in redemptive history, a focal point of mystical contemplation and aspiration: "God himself will be with them" (Rev 21:3). How does one even begin to comprehend such a thing? John does the best he can by using language recalling the ancient tabernacle in the wilderness of Sinai.

In describing the descent of the holy city, John uses the Greek word meaning "to tabernacle," deliberately recalling the temple's courtyard and sanctuary divided into a holy place and a most holy place. The last-named room was a perfect cube of 10 cubits (15 ft.), in which resided the Ark of the Covenant. Surmounting the lid like sentries stood two cherubim facing each other with outstretched wings. Above this lid, called the mercy seat, the divine presence (called the Shekinah in Jewish tradition), shimmered in a translucent cloud. Only the high priest was allowed access to the Most Holy place, and that only once a year on the solemn day of Yom Kippur. On that day, the high priest sprinkled the blood of a bull on the mercy seat with his finger seven times, thereby atoning for the sins of Israel (Lev 16:14). With the arrival of the New Jerusalem, the barriers between God and the church have been completely removed.

John's description of the holy city brings us full circle. In the garden of Eden, the first couple enjoyed unhindered communion with the Creator (see Gen 3:8). After their disobedience, the guilty couple were expelled and excluded from the garden. Communion with God was constrained and life must be lived east of Eden under a curse. Redemptive history can be likened to a tortuous journey back to the garden and the immediate presence of God. In the early stages of redemptive history, God occasionally revealed himself to patriarchs and matriarchs through dreams, visions and visible visitations (e.g., Gen 18). Following the exodus (Exod 1–18), God provided the people of Israel with tangible evidence of his presence by means of the tabernacle and its mysterious ark of the covenant overshadowed by a pillar of cloud by day and a pillar of fire by night (Exod 13:21; 19:9; 33:9; 40:34–38). Even so, access was guarded and limited—falling considerably short of the fellowship experienced in the garden.

The center point of redemptive history involved the mystery of incarnation in which the eternal Son took on human flesh and "lived among us" (lit. "tabernacled among us"; John 1:14; cf. 1 Tim 3:16). Having taken on human flesh, the Lamb of God made "the atoning sacrifice for our sins, and not for ours only but also for the sins of the whole world" says the apostle John (1 John 2:2; cf. Heb 1:3; 2:10–18; 7:26—8:6; 9:11–28). To be sure, the present age brings us much closer to the Father by means of the indwelling Christ and the Holy Spirit who takes up residence (lit. "tabernacles") in each believer (John 14:18–31; 16:12—17:25). In fact, Jesus reminds his disciples that "Whoever has seen me has seen the Father" (John 14:9). Paul makes the same point when he tells the Corinthian Christians that God gives them "the light of the knowledge of the glory of God in the face of Jesus Christ" (2 Cor 4:6). The writer to the Hebrews even exhorts his readers "to enter the sanctuary by the blood of Jesus" and "to approach with a true heart in full assurance of faith" (Heb 10:19, 22).

But we're still not home yet. As the writer of Hebrews later clarifies: "For here we have no lasting city, but we are looking for the city that is to come" (13:14). Now, in Rev 21–22, John depicts the glorious homecoming, the finish of a long journey. At long last, the distance between God and his people disappears: "They will see his face, and his name will be on their foreheads" (22:4). This climactic encounter is often called the beatific vision and fulfills the Master's promise to the pure in heart, "they will see God" (Matt 5:8).

John employs another striking metaphor to describe the splendor of this moment. He likens the New Jerusalem to "a bride adorned for her husband" (Rev 21:2). Weddings are grand occasions in all cultures and especially so in Jewish tradition. Great care was taken to present the bride as lovely as possible. Family jewels and heirlooms bedecked the bride and every effort was made to enhance her beauty and charm (Isa 61:10; Jer 2:32). Of course, she was dressed in fine, white linen as befitting a virgin. The symbolism conveys more good news in the book of Revelation: the church is the bride of Christ, resplendent in righteousness made possible through his atoning work on her behalf.

Life on the new earth and in the New Jerusalem is so radically different that John must resort to definition by negation, that is, describing what isn't present. Befitting the symbolism of perfection, seven aspects of the present fallen world are absent in the new creation. Here are the blessed subtractions of the age to come:

1. No more sea (Rev 21:1)

2. No more death (Rev 21:4a)

3. No more mourning, crying, and pain (Rev 21:4b)

4. No temple (Rev 21:22)

5. No night (Rev 21:25)

6. Nothing unclean (Rev 21:27)

7. Nothing accursed (Rev 22:3)

Note how numbers 1 and 5 speak to pre-creation deficiencies that were partially remedied by God's original creative acts, but are now completely removed in the new creation, namely, no more watery chaos and total darkness (Gen 1:2). Numbers 2, 3, 6, and 7 bring to fruition God's saving acts in redemptive history, namely, the redemption of body, soul, and spirit (1 Thess 5:23; Rom 8:18–30; Phil 3:20–21). Number 5, a rather unexpected absence, signals a quantum leap forward in the New Jerusalem: "I saw no temple in the city, for its temple is the Lord God the Almighty and the Lamb" (Rev 21:22). The immediate presence of the triune God is such that a temple is superfluous. The verdict is clear: "the first things have passed away" (Rev 21:4) and God is "making all things new" (Rev 21:5).

How fitting that the final description focuses on an enchanted garden. We walk back in time, as it were, to the celebrated garden of Eden— except this timeless garden exceeds in every way the glories and splendor of that primeval garden. The eschatological garden is nothing short of perfection and beggars by comparison the royal gardens of imperial Rome. Gracing the garden in the middle of the New Jerusalem is a crystal clear river coursing "from the throne of God and of the Lamb through the middle of the street of the city" (Rev 22:1–2). The tree of life flanks both sides of the river producing twelve kinds of fruit and leaves for the healing of the nations.

The paradise imagery conveys the reality of eternal life, fulfilling to the nth degree the mission of Jesus: "I have come that they may have life, and have it abundantly" (John 10:10). The integrity and security of the enchanted garden are failsafe: "Nothing accursed will be found there any more" (Rev 22:3). The world to come renders impossible a repeat performance of redemptive history or a recurring cycle of conflict and resolution. Note also the equal access all citizens enjoy to the water of life, the tree of life, and the source of all life: God himself. Not a whiff of class, gender, hierarchical, national, racial or social elitism, and prejudice may be detected in a place where each individual's name is written in the Lamb's book of life and each bears God's own name written on their foreheads. At last, justice and mercy for all prevails and both the sanctity of persons and the value of community are forever honored and preserved in the New Jerusalem.

But is it really too good to be true? Each reader must decide that question for themselves. The good news of Revelation can't be empirically, historically or logically proven. But the message is self-authenticating. Assurance arises within the heart of each person who accepts the divine testimony: "These words are trustworthy and true . . ." (Rev 22:6). And those who "listen to what the Spirit is saying" (Rev 2:7, 11, 17, 29; 3:6, 13, 22) know in the depths of their being that it is just as the Master said, "you will know the truth, and the truth will set you free" (John 8:32).

The story has run its course. The train of redemptive history has arrived at its final destination. As the glorious new creation fades from view, John, overcome with emotion, falls at the feet of his angelic guide to worship. For this he is sternly rebuked: "You must not do that!" (Rev 22:9). Echoing the creed of both Testaments (Exod 2:2–6; Deut 6:4–5, 14–15; Matt 6:24; 1 Cor 8:4–6; Col 2:8–10; 1 Tim 2:5), the angel enjoins John: "Worship God" (Rev 22:9). This in effect brings us full circle to the opening of the book, in which we are informed that this remarkable revelation has its ultimate source in the Alpha and Omega (Rev 1:1, 8). The Christ-centered message of Revelation is undergirded by a God-centered theology uniting both Old and New Testaments. The twenty-four elders before the throne of God give voice to this central affirmation of Scripture: "You are worthy, our Lord and God, to receive glory and honor and power, for you created all things, and by your will they existed and were created" (Rev 4:11).

The book of Revelation concludes with exhortation and warning. On the one hand, believers in Jesus Christ are exhorted to wait expectantly for his imminent return: "See, I am coming soon!" (Rev 22:7, 12, 20) and "the time is near" (Rev 22:10). This, too, brings us full circle to the opening announcement: "Look! He is coming with the clouds . . ." (Rev 1:7). John's first readers, the believers in the province of Asia, must not weaken in their resolve to follow the Lamb whatever the cost nor lose their grip on the hope of his soon return. Rewards and blessings of incalculable proportions are at stake (Rev 22:12–14). And the same is true for each generation of readers.

For those in the seven churches of Asia Minor who were weary with persecution and heartbreak, and for us who tire of the daily grind, the uncertainties of life, and the pain and loss of this world, the final outcome of Revelation is nothing short of astonishing. The worst parts of our world have been undone. The broken parts of our world have been completely recreated. The infection of evil has been rooted out and eradicated. Those opposed to the rule of God have been swept aside. All of creation has shifted:

- From Fear to Peace.

- From Uncertainty to Stability.

- From Violence to Safety.

- From Powerless to Powerful.

- From Injustice to Justice.

- From Pain to Comfort.

- From Hiding to inhabiting the Ends of the Earth.

In the Millenium, New Jerusalem, and the wedding feast that cap off the story of Revelation and the redemption story of Scripture, we find the fitting ending that we've desired all along. For every time we've seen suffering or evil in our world and said to ourselves, "That isn't right . . ." we'll finally fulfill the longing for justice that God has placed in our hearts. The dwelling of God is among his people, the kingdom of God is fully present, and every hope of Scripture has been fulfilled. The message of the good news is now a reality on earth as it is in heaven.